the buddha in your mirror

The Buddha in Your Mirror

PRACTICAL BUDDHISM
AND THE SEARCH FOR SELF

Woody Hochswender

Greg Martin

Ted Morino

MIDDLEWAY

PRESS

Published by Middleway Press
A division of the SGI-USA
606 Wilshire Blvd., Santa Monica, CA 90401

© 2001 SGI-USA

ISBN 0-9674697-1-6 (hardcover)
ISBN 0-9674697-8-3 (softcover)

Cover design by Lightbourne
Interior design by Gopa and the Bear

10   9   8   7   6   5   4   3   2

Library of Congress Cataloging-in-Publication Data

Hochswender, Woody, 1951–
    The Buddha in your mirror : practical Buddhism
and the search for self / Woody Hochswender,
Greg Martin, Ted Morino.
        p. cm.
    Includes bibliographical references and index.
    ISBN 0-9674697-1-6 (hardcover : alk paper)
    ISBN 0-9674697-8-3 (softcover : alk paper)
        1. Religious life—Soka Gakkai.
2. Nichiren, 1222—1282. I. Martin, Greg, 1950–
II. Morino, Ted, 1947– III. Title.

BQ8436.H63 2001
294.3'444—dc21   2001000679

Table of Contents

"No Butter Notes"

—a foreword by Herbie Hancock

WHY HAVE YOU, no matter what your realm of life, picked up this book? Even for a moment. Wouldn't you agree that no matter where we're at, we can always be at least a little happier? And while we may be feeling pretty good today, sometimes without warning or explanation, we just end up in a funk.

Even those of us who may appear to have been blessed in this life have our periods when the good things around us still don't allow us to live with joy. There has to be something more, something deeper.

But even when by all appearances things are going well, we often don't recognize that we are experiencing problems. When I think about the many contemporaries and friends in my profession who have come and gone, the legends who have passed from this life too soon, whose musical voices were silenced through losing the battle of illness or drugs, the need for a method to acquire lasting happiness is obvious.

The realities of the jazz life (and I'm sure it's the same for many occupations) are not easy. It takes a lot of strength, physical and spiritual, to tour constantly—sometimes traveling to a new country every day for months on end, to continue to tap one's creativity, to maintain healthy relationships. In the midst of life's stark realities, on both the professional and personal levels, it has been the profound, yet easy-to-grasp, life-affirming philosophy of Nichiren Buddhism that has sustained me for some twenty-nine years.

But let's back it up a bit.

I wasn't born into a rich family—in fact, we were quite poor. But I was fortunate in that we always had food on the table. Even more important, I had the support of parents who encouraged me to live my dreams. And they supported those dreams to the best of their ability. Though they couldn't afford to send me to college, they did anyway, somehow.

Along with the support of my parents, my life has largely been guided by various mentors I've had the fortune to encounter along the journey to today. Three of them especially stand out. The first was the second piano teacher I ever had—Mrs. Jordan.

Way back before jazz was a part of my consciousness, I was a nine-year-old boy with two years of piano study under my belt. This was in Chicago, 1949. I can't remember now how I was introduced to Mrs. Jordan, but to this day, I can't forget what she taught me. After hearing me play a bit she said that, yes, it was clear I could read music. But at that very first meeting she asked me if I was familiar with things like touch, nuance, phrasing—even how to breathe when I sat at the keyboard—concepts that were alien to my experience. When I said no, she said, "I'll show you." And she sat down and played a piece by Chopin that was so gorgeous my nine-year-old jaw dropped.

Mrs. Jordan taught me that playing the piano was so much more than just knowing the notes. Watching her play with such warmth, such dignity and such passion, I was able, without realizing it, to pick up the idea that the piano was an instrument for self-expression.

Through her honesty and continual efforts to find the means to explain to a young boy that which might otherwise remain ungraspable, Mrs. Jordan fired my desire to learn. And as a testament to her teaching abilities, in just about a year and a half, I won a major Chicago piano competition and got to play a concerto with the Chicago Symphony at Orchestra Hall.

Studying with Mrs. Jordan was the first time I remember seeing a new dimension in something seemingly familiar, and the impact of that has stayed with me all this time. In fact, I think that's what great mentors do; they excite within you a capacity to look at something in a new way, a way that resonates particularly within you. What I also got from Mrs. Jordan, without realizing it at the time, was a sense of how one person's sincerity could have a permanent impact on another.

Miles Davis was that kind of mentor, too. He was a singular character who was so fully the master of his instrument and his music that he solidly did things the way he felt they ought to be. Miles took a lot of flack for turning his back on audiences in performance. But those of us in his band saw clearly that he did that in order to direct us in subtle ways—a head shake here, a slight gesture with his horn there—as he continued his own virtuosic playing. Miles just forged ahead and never felt the need to explain himself.

Those of us who worked with and for Miles got a taste of his particular genius, which went beyond his playing. What was really special was his ability to draw all of us into the process and completely integrate whatever we brought to the table. He told us that he was paying us to do our practicing right there on the bandstand, that he was hiring us to create, to contribute something. And onstage or in the studio, he proved repeatedly that whatever we came up with, he could seize it and make something happen. On many occasions he saved our butts with this ability, turning our outright mistakes into musical themes he would instantly incorporate into whatever we were cooking.

And when we got stuck, he had the knack for getting us out of it — in his own peculiar way. Once, when I faced the musician's equivalent of writer's block, Miles leaned over and mumbled in my ear: "Put a B in the bass." A bit puzzled, I tried to work in what I thought he was talking about, and sure enough a spark started to happen, which fed him, which in turn fed me, leading to a musical dialogue.

Another time when I was in a rut, he dropped this on me: "Don't play the butter notes." That sent my mind reeling. Finally, I assumed he was telling me to somehow avoid the obvious. I'm not even sure to this day if Miles really knew what he meant, but I took it to mean remove the thirds and sevenths from the chords I was playing. Without getting too technical musically, let's just say this opened up the sound so that whomever I would be improvising with could make much more of a contribution to exploring the possibilities of a melody. Whatever Miles had in mind, the guidance worked — we caught fire! To me, that's an example of greatness in leadership. Instead of dictating, he stimulated me to find the solution within myself, the whole time supporting me with the full confidence that he could harmonize with all of us and get us to create harmony together.

Miles continually made us feel that each of us had something unique that only we could contribute. He did this with few words; it was mostly through his behavior. I couldn't fully realize this back then — I saw it only after I started my practice of Nichiren Buddhism.

Which leads me to the third mentor who impacted my life — Daisaku Ikeda. As president of the Soka Gakkai International, he has opened so many doors for twelve million people in 163 nations to gain access to the principles laid down in this book.

To me, Daisaku Ikeda is a man who encourages the creative expression of the individual, the harmonizing and blending of the peoples of the planet. He is working to attain peace, teaching everyone how to have at their fingertips the key to daily renewal, refreshment of spirit, happiness and the building of good fortune.

Applying the lessons in his myriad writings and

lectures on how to harness the power of Nam-myoho-renge-kyo—the mystic principle that drives the universe—I have knocked down wall after wall of obstacles in my life and seen the fulfillment of so many of my goals and dreams. I am solid in my conviction that I can handle whatever life throws at me.

As I developed happiness as the essence of my life, through Daisaku Ikeda's shining example of one who never gives up, never succumbs to negativity, I learned from him that any given moment can be looked at from an infinite number of perspectives. Among all those perspectives is the way to perceive a golden path within that moment and a way to perceive a diamond within each person. This impacts everything, from how I might put together certain music on a record I'm making—how I improvise—to how I look at the people I encounter in the various realms of my life. No matter what a person may be exhibiting at any given moment, it is only one part of a whole human being; each person contains the seed of enlightenment within and therefore deserves respect. While it's easy to forget that—especially when encountering the so-called difficult individuals one finds in the show business industry and elsewhere—Daisaku Ikeda's continual example and guidance stand as a means to measure my own behavior and to bring out a better side of others as I strive daily to improve myself.

Twenty-nine years of Buddhist practice have given me a solid foundation. Looking back, I have a take on my music that I'm, well, happy with. For me, the joy of playing music goes beyond the applause, the awards, the excitement of the fans. Of course that stuff's nice, but there's something that cuts much deeper. Working with music is more about letting yourself dig deep into your heart, about having the confidence to be vulnerable and to express that vulnerability, that core of your humanness, in an honest way. It's about being aware of your environment—the other musicians as well as the listeners. It's about pouring stuff out from the inside and manifesting it in the present—letting it flow from the most elevated part of your life. It's the process of doing all that not just for self-pleasure but with the sincere hope of moving something in the lives of others—helping them feel good about themselves, inspiring them to tap their possibilities and achieve their hopes for the present moment and their dreams for the future—to stimulate them to accomplish something great.

Woody Hochswender, Greg Martin and Ted Morino have done a terrific job putting together this book. These three gentlemen are also students of Daisaku Ikeda and have experienced the impact of Nichiren Buddhism by turning his guidance into action. *The Buddha in Your Mirror* puts Nichiren's profound concepts into readily accessible terms.

Whether you're reading this book out of mere curiosity or you have a crying need to elevate your life and circumstances, I encourage you to give the practical advice offered in *The Buddha in Your Mirror* a solid try. Perhaps the notion of Buddhism seems exotic or far off your own spiritual path. But if you're stuck in a rut, it's time to stop playing life's "butter notes" and open yourself up to seeing something new in the melody of life. What can you lose...except your blues?

The Buddha
in Your Mirror

ONE

THE
BUDDHA
IN YOUR
MIRROR

When deluded, one is called an ordinary being,
but when enlightened, one is called a Buddha.
This is similar to a tarnished mirror that will
shine like a jewel when polished.

—Nichiren

If there is any religion that could
cope with modern scientific needs
it would be Buddhism.

—Albert Einstein

BIRDS SING. The wind blows. The earth turns. Stars flare and die. Galaxies spin gracefully through space. Man is born, lives, grows old and dies. The patterns of existence are mysterious and immeasurable. Who can even begin to comprehend them? Our mundane daily lives are, in a way, no less complex. Who can always fathom, for example, the needs of a three-year-old child, let alone the inexplicable demands of one's in-laws or one's boss? During a single day, we rejoice at times while we despair at other times. Our feelings change from moment to moment. Trivial things can make us temporarily happy, while temporary setbacks can make us inexpressibly sad. Worries easily take the place of happiness. Life may be interpreted as a continual battle against problems large and small.

Never before in the history of the West have so many people turned to the timeless wisdom of Buddhism for answers to the great questions of life as well as to master the problems of daily existence. This is no coincidence, for we live in an age of experimentation and scientific inquiry, and Buddhism has no conflict with the world of science. Indeed, Buddhism has been called "the science of life."

Certainly the images and language of Buddhism have been surfacing with increasing regularity in contemporary culture, from movies and pop songs to magazines and television shows. There is the Buddha of the novel *The Buddha of Suburbia*, or the dharma of the TV sitcom, *Dharma and Greg*. The word *karma* has entered the Western vernacular and is blithely applied to everything from health-food shakes to nagging relationship problems. Everyone we don't particularly like or understand these days seems to have "bad karma." And there seems to be a Zen to everything, from playing golf to vanquishing your foes at office politics to perhaps even folding your laundry. Obi Wan Kenobi may not be portrayed as a Buddhist, per se, but his acumen in wielding the metaphysical Force of the epic *Star Wars* cycle, a mystic power that permeates the universe and ennobles its masters, resembles both the Buddhist concept of "life force" and the legendary powers attributed to the Buddhas in ancient scripture.

The actual meaning of these words, from the stand-point of Buddhist tradition, has become somewhat clouded. In the West, Buddhism has long been perceived as an elitist or beatnik religion, something to be discussed over espresso along with radical politics and difficult art. This lasting image perhaps stems from the Beat period of Jack Kerouac's *The Dharma Bums*, the explanatory books of Alan Watts and countless literary scenes featuring bongos and *satori* (the Japanese term for enlightenment used particularly in Zen). One could easily gain the impression that Buddhism is primarily a system of intellectual abstraction or a means of escaping from material reality. For many the overriding popular image of Buddhism is that of an abstruse and impenetrable mystical teaching studied in monkish isolation, the goal of which is inner peace as an end in itself. There is a famous story about the historical Buddha that demonstrates why this view is incorrect.

While walking one day in Deer Park in Benares, India, the Buddha came across a deer lying on the ground. A hunter's arrow had pierced its side. As the deer slowly died, two Brahmans, or holy men, stood over the body arguing over the exact time life leaves the body. Seeing the Buddha and wishing to resolve their debate, they asked his opinion. Ignoring them, the Buddha immediately approached the deer and drew out the arrow, saving the animal's life.

Buddhism is a beautiful philosophy, but above all, it is about action.

If the pop images and adaptations of Buddhism are sometimes offhand and imprecise, they nevertheless point to a surprising truth: The language and wisdom of Buddhism are increasingly being applied to the complexities of modern life because they actually seem to fit. Buddhist concepts and strategies, as applied to happiness, health, relationships, careers and even the process of aging and dying, pertain to the truth of modern existence — the actual pulsing reality of life. Buddhist ideas are entering the mainstream because they contain a descriptive power well adapted to the flux and flow of the modern world, without the weight of a dogmatic morality.

Buddhism explains the profound truths of life. But it also provides an immensely practical method for overcoming obstacles and transforming oneself. What you learn in these pages can be applied to every area of your existence: family, work, relationships, health. And it can be applied by anyone.

This book has the power to change your life. Although

it is not, strictly speaking, a self-help book, it includes the most time-honored and effective self-help secrets ever formulated—the all-embracing system of thought that is Buddhism. It is titled *The Buddha in Your Mirror* because of its most fundamental insight: the Buddha is *you*. That is, each and every human being contains the inherent capacity to be a *Buddha*, an ancient Indian word meaning "enlightened one," or one who is awakened to the eternal and unchanging truth of life.

By tapping into this vast inner potential, our Buddha nature, we find unlimited resources of wisdom, courage and compassion. Instead of avoiding or fearing our problems, we learn to confront them with joyful vigor, confident in our ability to surmount whatever life throws in our path. This latent potential could be likened to a rosebush in winter—the flowers are dormant even though we know that the bush contains the potential to bloom.

But on a day-to-day basis, this higher self, this enlightened state, is hidden from view; it is the proverbial "treasure too close to see." This fundamental aspect of the human predicament is illustrated in the Buddhist parable "The Gem in the Robe," as told in the Lotus Sutra. It is the story of a poor man who visits a wealthy friend:

The house was a very prosperous one
and [the poor man] was served many trays
    of delicacies.
The friend took a priceless jewel,
sewed it in the lining of the poor man's robe,
gave it without a word and then went away,
and the man, being asleep, knew nothing of it.
After the man had gotten up,
he journeyed here and there to other countries,
seeking food and clothing to keep himself alive,
finding it very difficult to provide for his livelihood.
He made do with what little he could get
and never hoped for anything finer,
unaware that in the lining of his robe
he had a priceless jewel.
Later the close friend who had given him the jewel
happened to meet the poor man
and after sharply rebuking him,
showed him the jewel sewed in the robe.
When the poor man saw the jewel,
his heart was filled with great joy,
for he was rich, possessed of wealth and goods
sufficient to satisfy the five desires.
We are like that man.

This parable depicts the blindness of human beings to the preciousness of their lives and the fundamental life-condition of Buddhahood. The purpose of this book is to help you discover this stunning jewel within and polish it till it shines brightly, illuminating not just your life but the lives of those around you. For Buddhism teaches that one's own awakening (or transformation) also has an immediate and far-reaching effect on his or her family, friends and society. This is a key point. When we reflect on the lessons of the twentieth century, stained by bloodshed and suffering, we must acknowledge that efforts to reform and restructure the institutions of society, to truly deepen human happiness, have come up short. Buddhism stresses inner, personal transformation as the way to promote lasting, sustainable resolutions to world problems.

So what does it mean to be a Buddha? The word *Buddha* was a common noun used in India during the lifetime of Shakyamuni, the historical Buddha. This is an important point in the sense that enlightenment is not regarded as the exclusive province of one individual. The Buddhist sutras talk of the existence of Buddhas other than Shakyamuni. In a sense, then, Buddhism comprises not only the teaching of the Buddha but also the teaching that enables all people to become Buddhas.

The Life of the Buddha

Unlike the Western religions of Judaism, Christianity and Islam, Buddhism makes no claim of divine revelation. Instead, it is the teaching of a single human being who, through his own efforts, awoke to the law of life within himself. He was a man who wrote nothing down and about whom we know very little—but what is known has become the catalyst for changing millions of lives.

The historical Buddha, whose given name was Siddhartha (One Who Has Achieved His Goal) and family name was Gautama (Best Cow), was born in Northern India approximately 2,500 TO 3,000 years ago. Opinions differ as to the actual date, but modern research tends to place the Buddha's birth in either the sixth or fifth century B.C.E. The timing, while not exact, remains significant. As the German philosopher Karl Jaspers has noted, Siddhartha was born at approximately the same time as Socrates in Greece, Confucius in China and Isaiah in the Judaic world. The simultaneous appearance of these great men, according to Jaspers, marked the dawn of spiritual civilization.

Siddhartha's father was the ruler of the Shakya clan, a small tribe located near the border of Nepal, hence the

Buddha came to be known as Shakyamuni (Sage of the Shakyas). Since the written record is scant, the details of his early life are sketchy. We know that Siddhartha was born a prince and lived in affluence. And we know that he was endowed with keen intelligence and an introspective nature. As a young man, he took a wife, Yashodhara, who bore him a son, Rahula. Eventually he forsook his wealthy, privileged existence to pursue a path of wisdom and self-knowledge. What drove him to leave the luxury of home and the security of family is expressed in the legend of the four meetings.

The young prince is said to have left his palace in Kapilavastu on four different occasions. Exiting from the eastern gate, he encountered a man bent and shriveled with age. Leaving through the southern gate, he saw a sick person. On a third outing, emerging from the western gate, he saw a corpse. Finally, going out through the northern gate, he came upon a religious ascetic. The old man, the sick person and the corpse represent the problems of old age, sickness and death. Together with birth (or living itself), these conditions are called the "four sufferings"—the fundamental problems of human existence. Shakyamuni's motive in abandoning his princely status for an ascetic life was nothing less than to discover how to overcome the four sufferings.

In the manner of ancient Indian *arhats,* or holy men, who wandered the countryside in quest of ultimate truth, Siddhartha began his journey. We know that the path was arduous and filled with physical and mental challenges. He first traveled south and entered Rajagriha, capital of the kingdom of Magadha, where he practiced under the teacher Alara Kalama, who, through meditation, was said to have attained "the realm where nothing exists." Quickly attaining the same stage, Siddhartha found his questions unresolved. He turned to another sage, Uddaka Ramaputta, who had attained "the realm where there is neither thought nor no thought." Mastering this meditation as well, Siddhartha still had not found answers to his deepest questions.

As Daisaku Ikeda, one of the foremost modern interpreters of Buddhism, has written in *The Living Buddha:* "For yoga masters like Alara Kalama and Uddaka Ramaputta, yoga practice had become an end in itself…. Both yoga and Zen meditation are excellent practices developed by Asian philosophy and religion, but, as Shakyamuni made clear, they should be employed as methods for attaining an understanding of the ultimate truth, not looked upon as ends in themselves."

Siddhartha then embarked on a series of ascetic practices, including temporary suspension of breathing,

fasting and mind control. After several years of tormenting his body almost to the point of death, he finally aban-
doned the rigorous ascetic pursuits that had debilitated
him and proceeded to meditate under a pipal, a type of
fig tree (later named the bodhi tree) near Gaya. Eventually, around the age of thirty, he attained enlightenment and became a Buddha.

The Buddha's Enlightenment

It is impossible to know exactly what the Buddha realized beneath that tree. But based on his many teachings,
which, like Homer's *Odyssey*, were first orally transmit-
ted by his followers, we know that sitting under the pipal
tree he attempted to reach beyond ordinary consciousness to a place where he perceived himself as one with
the life of the universe.

It has been recorded that in the early stages of his
meditation he was still bound by the distinction between
subject (himself) and object (exterior world). He was
aware of his own consciousness being surrounded by a
wall—the boundary of his body as well as the environment outside of himself. Finally, according to Daisaku
Ikeda in *The Living Buddha*:

Shakyamuni had a clear vision of his own life in all its manifestations in time. According to the doctrine of transmigration, which had from early times been expounded in Brahmanism, the life of a human being is by no means something limited to the present. Shakyamuni, meditating under the Bodhi tree, clearly recollected all his previous existences one by one, and perceived that his present existence was part of the unbroken chain of birth, death, and rebirth that had been continuing through incalculable eons in the past.

This was not something that came to him as a kind of intuition, nor did he perceive it as a concept or idea. It was a clear and real recollection— not unlike, though on a very different plane from, the events deeply buried within the recesses of our mind that we suddenly remember when we are in a state of extreme tension or concentration.

He understood the true aspect of reality as "impermanence." So what does this mean?

All things, all phenomena are undergoing constant change. Life, nature and society never cease to change for even a single moment. It looks as if the desk you are sitting at or the book you hold in your hands or the building you live in are solidly constructed. But they will all crumble someday. Buddhism clearly explains that suffering emerges in our hearts because we forget the principle of impermanence and believe that what we possess will last forever.

Suppose you have a good-looking girlfriend or boyfriend. Do you spend a lot of time wondering what she or he will look like in thirty or forty years? Of course not. It is human nature to feel that health and youth will last forever. Similarly, there are few wealthy people who imagine that their money could someday be gone. There is nothing wrong with people thinking this way. Nevertheless, we suffer because we have such notions. You may want to keep your sweetheart young and beautiful forever and may make intensive efforts toward making love last. Still, if and when the time comes to depart from your loved one, you will feel the deepest pain. Because people want to accumulate wealth, some will go so far as to struggle against others; and if they lose that wealth, they must taste the bitter fruit of suffering. Even the attachment to life itself entails suffering, because we fear death. Buddhism teaches us to recognize these cycles of impermanence and have the courage to accept them.

In addition to his understanding of impermanence, the interrelatedness of all things is said to have unfolded in

Shakyamuni's awakened mind. The universe and everything in it are in flux, arising and ceasing, appearing and disappearing, in an unending cycle of change conditioned by the law of causation. All things are subject to the law of cause and effect, and consequently nothing can exist independently of other things. This Buddhistic concept of causation is also known as "dependent origination." Shakyamuni awakened to the eternal law of life that permeates the universe, the mystic aspect of life in which all things in the universe interrelate and influence one another in an unending cycle of birth and death.

The substance of Shakyamuni's awakening is explained in the concept of the Four Noble Truths, which explains that (1) all existence is suffering; (2) suffering is caused by selfish craving; (3) the eradication of selfish craving brings about the cessation of suffering and enables one to attain nirvana; and (4) there is a path by which this eradication can be achieved, namely, the discipline of the eightfold path. Here we can see the earliest indications that the process of achieving absolute happiness emancipated from the sufferings of life is a path or journey.

Dispelling ignorance and establishing a correct view are the centerpiece of Buddhist practice. They are also the motivation that initiated a three-thousand-year search — beginning with Shakyamuni himself — to elucidate the vehicle (or method) that would carry a Buddhist practitioner along the path to the cessation of suffering and the attainment of absolute happiness. All of the various Buddhist schools and practices have developed in an effort to create such a vehicle.

For some time following his awakening, Shakyamuni remained seated under the bodhi tree in a joyful state. When he re-entered the world, however, he soon began to be troubled by the thought that his enlightenment to the law of life might prove difficult to communicate. Since the depth of his understanding greatly surpassed that of the most advanced spiritual seekers of his day, he prepared his listeners by first instructing them with easy-to-understand parables and analogies. In this way, Shakyamuni gradually awakened those he taught, while adhering to his ultimate aim of showing all people that they possess Buddhahood.

As he states in a telling passage from the Lotus Sutra:

At all times I think to myself:
How can I cause living beings
to gain entry into the unsurpassed way
and quickly acquire the body of a Buddha?

It was no easy task. Shakyamuni spent the remaining forty-some years of his life preaching to troubled people in ways best suited to their understanding. In this light, we see that the idea of Buddhism as the special preserve of holy men meditating on mountaintops is erroneous. Shakyamuni never meant for his teachings to apply only to a cloistered group of devotees. All the evidence suggests that he wished for his teachings to become widespread and to be adopted by the common man — and woman. His lessons were compiled as the so-called eighty-four thousand teachings, which, like the teachings of Jesus, have been interpreted and re-interpreted for centuries. Indeed, the principal problem for Buddhists throughout the millennia has been not so much what the Buddha said but how to put his teachings into practice. How, in essence, to experience the Buddha's enlightenment, his transcendent wisdom. How to become a Buddha oneself.

The Road to Enlightenment

Today there are many schools of Buddhism, perhaps even thousands. The British scholar Christmas Humphreys once wrote: "To describe [Buddhism] is as difficult as describing London. Is it Mayfair, Bloomsbury, or the Old Kent Road? Or is it the lowest common multiple of all these parts, or all of them and something more?"

As the Buddhist philosophy gently flowed from India —north through China and Tibet, south into Thailand and Southeast Asia—it tended to absorb and be influenced by local religious customs and beliefs. The Buddhism that spread to Tibet and China and eventually to Korea and Japan was called Mahayana, meaning "greater vehicle." That which spread southward to Southeast Asia and Sri Lanka was called Hinayana, for "lesser vehicle," a pejorative term applied by the Mahayanists. The Hinayana schools, based on the earlier teachings of Shakyamuni, typically emphasized a strict and highly detailed code of personal conduct geared toward one's personal salvation. (The only Hinayana school today is Theravada, or "Teaching by the Elders.")The Mahayana schools emphasized the need for Buddhism to be a compassionate means for common people to attain enlightenment—to search for a practical method that could serve as a vehicle for greater numbers (the greater vehicle) to make the journey to Buddhahood.

The profusion of different Buddhist sutras and theories came to be a source of great confusion, particularly in China in the first and second centuries. At that time, Chinese scholars were confronted with the random introduction of the various sutras of the many Hinayana schools as well as the Mahayana scriptures. Perplexed by these diverse teachings, Chinese Buddhists attempted to compare and classify the sutras.

By the fifth century, the systematizing of the Buddhist canon had become very advanced. In particular, a Buddhist monk named Chih-i, later known as the Great Teacher T'ien-t'ai, developed the definitive standard known as "the five periods and eight teachings." Based on his own enlightenment, which may have rivaled Shakyamuni's, T'ien-t'ai's system classified the sutras chronologically as well as from the standpoint of profundity. He determined that the Lotus Sutra, the penultimate teaching of Shakyamuni expounded toward the end of his life, contained the ultimate truth. T'ien-t'ai formulated this truth as the principle of "three thousand realms in a single moment of life." It employs a phenomenological approach, describing all the kaleidoscopic emotions and mental states that human beings are subject to at any given moment. The theory of three thousand realms in a single moment of life holds that all the innumerable phenomena of the universe are encompassed in a single moment of a common mortal's life. Thus the macrocosm is contained within the microcosm.

The vast dimension of life to which Shakyamuni awoke under the bodhi tree was beyond the reach of ordinary human consciousness. T'ien-t'ai described this ultimate truth as three thousand realms in a single moment of life, recognizing that the Lotus Sutra was the only sutra to assert that all people — men and women, good and evil, young and old — had the potential to attain Buddhahood within their lifetimes.

A crucial question remained: How could common people apply this to their lives? Toward that end, T'ien-t'ai advocated a rigorous practice of observing the mind through meditation, delving deeper and deeper until the ultimate truth of three thousand realms in a single moment of life was grasped. Unfortunately, this type of practice was feasible only for monks, who could spend indefinite periods of time contemplating the message implicit in the Lotus Sutra. It was almost impossible for people who worked for a living and had other things on their minds. The full flowering of Buddhism was not to be accomplished until it migrated along trading routes to Japan. It would not be widely practiced and revered today without the incredible courage and insight of a thirteenth-century Japanese monk named Nichiren, who brought the Lotus Sutra into sharp focus in a way that had a direct impact on people and their daily lives.

Modern-Day Buddhism

Nichiren, born in Japan in 1222, gave concrete and practical expression to the Buddhist philosophy of life that Shakyamuni taught and T'ien-t'ai illuminated. He expressed the heart of the Lotus Sutra, and therefore the Buddha's enlightenment, in a form that all people could practice. He defined this as the invocation of Nam-myoho-renge-kyo, based on the title of the Lotus Sutra.

His achievement was akin to translating a complex scientific theory into a practical technique. Just as Benjamin Franklin's discovery of electricity was not harnessed for practical use until many years later when Thomas Edison invented the light bulb, Shakyamuni's enlightenment was inaccessible for all but a few until Nichiren taught the fundamental practice by which all people could call forth the law of life from within themselves. His realization of this principle had the power to directly affect and move the people who encountered it, heralding a new epoch in the history of Buddhism.

He had revealed the ultimate Mahayana teaching — the greater vehicle — by which all people could journey to Buddhahood. In Nichiren's own words, "A blue fly, if it clings to the tail of a thoroughbred horse, can travel ten thousand miles, and the green ivy that twines around the tall pine can grow to a thousand feet." For the first time, ordinary people could take a journey previously possible only for saints and sages.

Nichiren's Buddhism has proved itself to be of profound value to millions of people. It was Nichiren who expressed the essence of the Lotus Sutra in a way that enables all people, regardless of their level of knowledge, to enter the gateway to enlightenment. This was a revolutionary development in the history of religion.

While Buddhism began with the teaching of one human being who awoke to the law of life within himself, it has come to include the interpretations of that teaching by subsequent scholars and prophets. As we have said, the word *Buddha* originally meant "enlightened one," one who is awakened to the eternal truth or law of life (dharma). This truth is eternal and boundless. It is present always and everywhere. In this sense, the law of life is not the exclusive property of Shakyamuni Buddha or of Buddhist monks.

The truth is open equally to everyone. In the Buddhism described on these pages, there are no priests or gurus, no ultimate authority that decides what is correct or incorrect, what is right or wrong. In this Buddhism, the wall between priesthood and laity has been torn down, leading to a complete democratization of the practice. Because it is essentially nondogmatic, it suits the skeptics among us. The ultimate and all-abiding law that the Buddha perceived may be another name for some people's concept of God. On the other hand, a person who cannot believe in an anthropomorphic God can see an underlying energy to the universe. The breadth of Buddhism encompasses both views and focuses on the individual.

There is no external source to blame—and no one to implore for salvation. In Buddhism, no God or supernatural entity plans and shapes our fates. In Western religion, you can bring yourself closer to God through your faith, but you can never become God. In Buddhism, one could never be separate from the wisdom of God, because the ultimate wisdom already exists in the heart of every person. Through Buddhist practice, we seek to call forth that portion of the universal life force existing originally and eternally within—what we call Buddhahood—and manifest it by becoming a Buddha. Buddhists become aware of the existence, in their innermost depths, of the eternal law that permeates both the universe and the individual human being. They aim to live every day in accordance with that law. In so doing, they discover a way of living that redirects all things toward hope, value and harmony. It is the discovery of this objective law itself, as it manifests within the individual, that creates spiritual value, not some exterior power or being. As Nichiren stated in a famous letter titled "On Attaining Buddhahood In This Lifetime":

> Your practice of the Buddhist teachings will not relieve you of the sufferings of birth and death in the least unless you perceive the true nature of your life. If you seek enlightenment outside yourself, then your performing even ten thousand practices and ten thousand good deeds will be in vain. It is like the case of a poor man who spends night and day counting his neighbor's wealth but gains not even half a coin.

This idea that the power to achieve happiness lies totally within can be disconcerting. It entails a radical sense of responsibility. As Daisaku Ikeda has written: "Society is complex and harsh, demanding that you struggle hard to survive. No one can make you happy. Everything depends on you as to whether or not you attain happiness…. A human being is destined to a life of great suffering if he is weak and vulnerable to his external surroundings."

But far from being a bleak, nihilistic approach to life, the Buddhist practice and philosophy are filled with hope and practical solutions to the problems of everyday existence. The philosophy described in this book is so practical that we generally do not refer to it as a "religion" (although it is one) but as a "practice," because most of the people who follow it have found it to be extremely useful. So throughout this book, although there will be numerous discussions of the theory and philosophy of modern Buddhism, the emphasis will be on how you, the individual, can use Buddhism as a powerful tool to solve the problems of daily life.

As Nichiren quoted from the Lotus Sutra, "No worldly affairs are ever contrary to the true reality," and furthermore, "all phenomena in the universe are manifestations of the Buddhist law." In other words, daily life is the dramatic stage on which the battle for enlightenment is won or lost. Nichiren taught that common mortals, without eradicating their desires or changing their identity, could attain Buddhahood right here in this world. In an age of skepticism and widespread distrust of traditional faiths and institutions, such a dynamic, self-directed religious practice becomes all the more valuable.

Buddhism is essentially nonauthoritarian, democratic, scientific and based on insights obtained primarily through individual efforts toward self-perfection. But Buddhism also has immediate and far-reaching effects on the society around us. Buddhism is a way of life that makes no distinction between the individual human being and the environment in which that person lives. In its concept of the interrelatedness of all life forms in a complex web beyond complete human understanding, Buddhism has provided a spiritual and intellectual framework for environmental awareness. The Western worldview, as expounded by Christianity and Judaism, tends to be anthropocentric, placing humanity at the apex of the natural order. Buddhism on the other hand views humankind as a part of nature, supporting and giving rise to the notion of bioethics. Since every individual is connected to everything on earth, the destiny of our planet is influenced by the individual's actions.

Modern Buddhism is also nonmoralistic. In a world characterized by a great diversity of peoples, cultures and lifestyles, Buddhism does not prescribe one way of living. There are no "commandments." Buddhism accepts you exactly as you are, with all your foibles and misdemeanors, past and present. However, this does not mean you may lie, steal or murder. Buddhism depends for its moral force not on a list of rules for behavior but on an irresistible inner transformation. Buddhist practitioners find themselves acting more gently, compassionately and with absolute regard for the preciousness of other people's lives. This process becomes almost automatic.

Buddhism and the Cosmos

Finally, nothing of what the historical Buddha taught contradicts in any serious way the discoveries of Galileo and Einstein, Darwin and Freud. Yet his ideas were formed thousands of years before, without the aid of telescopes, high technology or even the written word. The Buddhist model of the universe strongly resembles the cosmology accepted today. While the Buddha never talked in terms of a "Big Bang," he nevertheless postulated a cosmos that is theoretically consistent with what many scientists now propose. In fundamental ways, Buddhist theory accepts the vast dimensions and space–time concepts of modern physics and is even congruent with the more abstruse realms of quantum theory. Articles on the latest breakthroughs in particle physics, for example, bear a remarkable resemblance to the doctrine of impermanence as expounded by the Buddha. In the Lotus Sutra, the central text of Mahayana Buddhism, a Promethean-scale view of the universe is articulated in the form of what is called a "major world system," a sweeping concept that implies both the existence of innumerable galaxies and the possibility of sentient life on planets outside our own. At the same time, it contains a detailed analysis of life that penetrates the depths of the human psyche. Thus Mahayana Buddhism takes as a basic premise the existence of numerous life-bearing worlds throughout the universe, while at the same time describing Buddhism as the driving force that enables individual human beings to bring about their own spiritual reformation, thereby assuring eternal peace and the long-term survival of civilizations.

Throughout its twenty-five-hundred-year history, the spread of Buddhism has been characterized by tolerance, gentleness and love of nature. As the French scholar Sylvain Levi stated, "Buddhism is justified in laying claim to the honor of having conquered a portion of the world without ever having resorted to violence and without ever having resorted to force of arms." In fact, the goal of Buddhists, and an underlying aim of this book, is world peace. In Buddhism, we say, "world peace through individual enlightenment." A peaceful and secure society will result through a process of individual dialogue—person by person by person—until war and its underlying causes vanish from the earth. For all these reasons, Buddhism is set to play a dynamic role in the emerging scientific culture of the twenty-first century.

With that shimmering idea as a backdrop, we will now turn to the idea of individual practice, including the secret law Nichiren discovered hidden in the depths of the Lotus Sutra. Because, before we can change the destiny of the world, we must first change ourselves.

TWO

THE
PRACTICE

To be a philosopher is not merely
to have subtle thoughts, nor even
to found a school.... It is to solve
some of the problems of life,
not theoretically, but practically.
—Henry David Thoreau

There's no way out of this mess,
except to become enlightened
and then enjoy it.
—Robert Thurman

A SWAN SEEMS to swim calmly, but under the water, invisible to us, it paddles unceasingly. Similarly, the Buddhist has a vigorous daily practice that, while not effortless, smoothes the way for things to go right in life. It enables one to approach the travails of existence with equanimity and poise. Enlightenment, or awareness of the universal truth underlying all phenomena, brings out the noblest and most rewarding aspects of a person's life.

What then is the correct daily practice of Buddhism that enables one to progress toward enlightenment?

Amid the symphony of change in the world outside, life changes from moment to moment. Even the chair you sit on is changing, at the molecular level, although the changes may be imperceptible to you. This constant change or fluctuation, expressed by the Buddhist concept of "impermanence," gives rise to the fundamental sufferings of human existence. But occasionally amid the flux of life, perhaps for a fleeting instant, we sense an underlying rhythm, a hum or a pulse, to all things. Such moments of insight and realization often occur after an experience of extraordinary beauty and tranquility, for example, contemplating a perfect Caribbean sunset while on vacation. Or such a moment might occur during a peak performance, perhaps scaling the face of a sheer rock wall, playing an intricate concerto, or catching a perfectly thrown pass just beyond the reach of two defenders. When such a moment occurs, it's like being in a special zone, where the unpredictable world outside and the turbulent world within merge, time is suspended, and we suddenly feel there's nothing we can't do.

But how do we make these peak moments happen whenever we want them to happen? How do we tap into this well of energy and wisdom when our own lives and the life of the universe seem, briefly, to be vibrating to the same wonderful tune?

The Buddhist teacher Nichiren, who lived and wrote in the thirteenth century, defined this rhythm, this underlying pulse of life, as Nam-myoho-renge-kyo. It enables everyone to tap into this limitless potential, this higher life-condition, at will. We call this higher state of life Buddhahood. In the writings of Nichiren, enlightenment is not a finite destination, a near-impossible goal to be

pursued lifetime after lifetime in an endless drama bor-
rowed from Sisyphus. Rather, it is an immanent quality,
present at all times in all life, waiting to be awakened at
any given moment.

According to this Buddhist teaching, each of us possesses the potential for happiness. Within us is the ability to live with courage, to have fulfilling relationships,
to enjoy good health, to show compassion for others, and
to face and surmount our deepest problems. To live this
sort of winning life, the individual must undergo an inner
transformation. This process involves a transformation of
our very character, an individual "human revolution."

Consider the following scenario: Perhaps you feel
underappreciated at work. Maybe your boss is belliger-
ent or ignores you. After a while, you develop a chip on
your shoulder. Though you may be an expert at hiding
negativity, every once in a while it rears its ugly head.
Perhaps your coworkers or boss perceive you in turn as
not being entirely committed to your job, or perhaps they
sense that you have a bad attitude. Of course, there are
myriad reasons for your attitude, all of them "valid." But
whatever the reasons, you miss opportunities for advancement because of the poor relationship. This is a
common scenario in today's working environment.

But suppose you start coming to work with a new

attitude that is not just a mental adjustment but an outlook bolstered by a deep sense of vitality, confidence and
compassion. Your compassion leads you to have empa-
thy for your boss's situation. Armed with understanding,
you treat your boss differently, offering support and finding yourself less and less discouraged by any negativity
he or she may display toward you. Your boss begins to see
you in a new light. Opportunities present themselves.

This is obviously a very simple example and seemingly simple to do. But to live this way every day requires a
basic change of heart. Once the change is made, like a
never-ending domino effect, we can have a continual
positive impact on the people around us. The catalyst
for experiencing this inner revolution is the practice of
Buddhism as taught by Nichiren, who stated that one
can achieve these results and much more simply by
chanting Nam-myoho-renge-kyo.

This basic Buddhist practice, established by Nichiren, consists of chanting the phrase Nam-myoho-renge-
kyo to the Gohonzon, a scroll inscribed with Chinese
and Sanskrit characters. (It is not necessary to have a
Gohonzon to begin practicing Buddhism, but millions
of people do. More about this later.) One chants Nam-
myoho-renge-kyo to achieve enlightenment, of course;
but it can also be chanted with the intention of gaining

happiness, personal growth, to improve your health or more temporal goals, like solving the professional impasse described above. In fact, you can chant for whatever you want.

You can chant for a better job — or to succeed at the one you are in. You can even chant to find a career if you do not have one. You can chant to find a mate, or you can chant to get along better with the significant other you already have. You can also chant to stave off depression, to overturn feelings of despair. In fact, most Buddhists chant on a daily basis for a number of things, from improving their own character to having a more peaceful environment. But in each instance, the Buddhist prayer is ultimately directed at revealing the practitioner's inherent Buddhahood, the highest state of life. How did Nichiren come upon this concrete and efficient formula for achieving life's dreams?

Like Shakyamuni Buddha before him, Nichiren wished to lead all people to enlightenment. In many schools of Buddhism, enlightenment seems remote and the process of attaining it an almost superhuman feat — something to be reached only after many lifetimes of patient effort. The traditional Buddhist strategies have included rigid austerities, some including strict dietary and lifestyle changes. Throughout history, Buddhists have retreated from life, to the forests, mountains and monasteries. But nowadays, relinquishing one's job and daily routine to go on a prolonged spiritual retreat—even if it's just for a weekend—is not an option for most. Nor is it practical for most people to devote themselves on a periodic basis to the monastic life, traveling to India, for instance, once or twice a year. Nichiren, in the thirteenth century, found a way to shorten the journey.

Nichiren and the Lotus Sutra

From the age of twelve, Nichiren, the son of a fisherman, began to study the sutras, vowing to become "the wisest man in all Japan." Born on February 16, 1222, he lived in a time of great religious ferment and political turmoil, when feudal lords vied for power and Japan was ruled by hereditary shoguns. In the thirteenth century, Japan was suffering through plagues, political instability, earthquakes and the imminent threat of foreign invasion. At sixteen, Nichiren was ordained a monk and began a serious comparison study of the confusing array of Buddhist teachings, particularly those of the Tendai sect, based on the teachings of the Chinese sage T'ien-t'ai. He also examined the Pure Land and Zen teachings, which had spread rapidly in the period of social turmoil following the decline of the imperial aristocracy and the rise of the samurai class. The Pure Land teachings became very popular among the general public, while Zen gained popularity among the samurai. Nichiren, however, clearly understood that most people remain unaware of their own Buddha nature, and even if they accept the idea in principle, have nary a clue as to how to activate it in their daily lives.

While Nichiren recognized T'ien-t'ai's accomplishment in classifying the sutras and, in particular, establishing the Lotus Sutra as supreme, he realized that the prescribed meditation methods were beyond the capacity of common people. He also noted that the lives of the priests he saw in the various sects, from the temples of Kyoto to the monasteries of Mount Hiei, were especially degraded. They vied with one another for fame and profit. They eventually began to seek political power and grow distant from the public. No wonder, then, that Buddhism had been unable to help people find happiness in their daily lives.

On April 28, 1253, Nichiren first declared Nam-myoho-renge-kyo to be the one true law, the great "secret" hidden in the depths of the Lotus Sutra. On the surface, he used *Myoho-renge-kyo*, the Japanese reading of the characters of the title of the Lotus Sutra, as translated by the linguist Kumarajiva from Sanskrit to Chinese, to express the idea of enlightenment, adding the word *nam*, meaning "devotion to." From a deeper perspective, he made Shakyamuni's enlightenment, expressed conceptually in the Lotus Sutra, accessible for the first time to all. This was an enormous advance in the history of Buddhism, not to mention the start of a revolution in the idea of religion itself.

The Buddhism of Nichiren does not require the renunciation or suppression of human desires. This was a fundamental change in outlook from other schools, which insist on the extinguishing of earthly desires to attain higher wisdom. Nichiren stated that the source of all desire is life itself; as long as life continues, we instinctively want to live, to cherish love, to seek profit, and so on. Since desire arises from the innermost core of life, it is virtually indestructible. Even the thirst for enlightenment is a kind of desire.

Civilization advanced because of the instincts and desires of men and women. The pursuit of wealth produced economic growth. The will to defy winter cold led to the development of natural science. Love, which is a basic human desire, inspired literature.

Not only can we fulfill our desires as we change ourselves from within, but also the desires themselves begin to change. They become purified or elevated. And the desires that we do have serve as fuel, propelling us toward our enlightenment. Followers of Nichiren chant morning and evening for their personal desires against the backdrop of the larger desires for individual enlightenment and world peace. This process of inner human revolution—the transformation of desires—is inextricably entwined with the reformation of the surrounding environment. Buddhists work tirelessly to bring peace and harmony to their jobs, families and communities while they struggle tenaciously to manifest the law from within. No one needs to go to the mountaintop. But every day we climb. Morning and evening, Buddhists climb the mountain of enlightenment through Buddhist practice in their own homes.

In terms of ancient Indian religious conventions, the phrase Nam-myoho-renge-kyo would be described as a mantra, and the Gohonzon, or scroll to which one directs the chant, as a mandala. But the Nichiren Buddhist practice is anything but a passive form of meditation; rather, it is a dynamic expression of mind and spirit. The results can manifest themselves in ways both subtle and dramatic. To take an example: In Tina Turner's autobiography, *I, Tina* (basis of the film *What's Love Got to Do With It?*), she describes her inability to summon the inner strength to escape the long-term abuse and brutality of her husband. This is a well-known story and analogous to situations in our own lives in which we feel totally trapped. Nothing seems to work; there is no apparent way out of our suffering and circumstances. But after an acquaintance teaches Tina to chant Nam-myoho-renge-kyo, she immediately begins to battle back. Conquering her own timidity, Tina strikes out to gain her freedom. Eventually, of course, she launches a fabulously successful independent career. In this instance, chanting Nam-myoho-renge-kyo galvanized her into action, giving her the impetus to change her destiny for the better. Her overriding need was not for inner peace but for outward determination. In countless cases, Buddhist practitioners substitute an attitude of joyous struggle for one of infinite resignation.

In many forms of meditation, it can be difficult to discern whether we are meditating correctly—or even if we are meditating at all. We easily lose our focus on the breath or mantra. The mind can easily be distracted by worries, fantasies and other thoughts. In contrast, chanting serves to focus the mind. One chants Nam-myoho-renge-kyo in a steady, vigorous rhythm (but not so loud as to disturb the neighbors or give one's roommate a headache).

It may seem strange at first, but it is definitely concrete. Anyone can actually just do it. You can try it yourself. Repeat the phrase out loud three times, as softly or as vigorously as you like. (For a guide to pronunciation and rhythm, see Chapter 8.) When you try this, believe it or not, you have already taken a significant step on the path to enlightenment.

What's Nam-myoho-renge-kyo Got To Do With It?

The question immediately arises: How can chanting a phrase that you understand barely, if at all, have any effect, positive or negative, on your life? The analogy Buddhists often use is to compare Nam-myoho-renge-kyo to milk. A baby is nourished by mother's milk and later by cow's milk long before the baby understands what *milk* means. The nutritional benefits are intrinsic to the milk. To use another example, we do not need to know how an automobile works in order to use it to get somewhere. It makes sense to learn a bit about how a car works, and study is an important part of a well-rounded Buddhist practice. But it is important to realize that the chant works whether you understand it or not, whether you believe it works or not. In fact, many people begin chanting Nam-myoho-renge-kyo with the express intent of proving to friends that it doesn't work—and, invariably, they are surprised to find out that it does. Nam-myoho-renge-kyo works for everyone, old and young, rich and poor, skeptical and gullible, ignorant and astute, African and Asian, Republican or Democrat or Whig.

According to Nichiren Buddhism, Nam-myoho-renge-kyo is the law of the universe, and by chanting it you reveal the law in your own life, putting yourself in harmony or rhythm with the universe. The word *law* here is used in the scientific sense, like the law of gravity. Since gravity is a law of life, it affects us whether we comprehend its workings or not. If you walked off the edge of a cliff prior to 1666, when Sir Isaac Newton formulated this law, you would still have suffered the consequences. Nam-myoho-renge-kyo is also a law of life, Nichiren said. In fact, it is *the* law of life. How could this be?

To begin to grasp this point, it might be helpful to consider Nam-myoho-renge-kyo in the light of Einstein's special theory of relativity, expressed by the famous equation $E=mc^2$. This is a foundation stone of our view of the cosmos. But do we really understand it? We know that E stands for energy and m for mass. Mass is multiplied by the speed of light squared, c^2. Though general readers may have only a vague sense of what these terms mean, they are well aware that the symbols Einstein used —E, m, c—stand for concepts of physics and mathematics that, although abstract, relate to the realities of time, space, energy and matter in our world. The same holds true for each of the characters in Nam-myoho-renge-kyo.

Though the meaning of $E=mc^2$ eludes us, nearly everyone these days is willing to admit the validity of Einstein's equation because it has been demonstrated innumerable times in the real world. Early in his career Einstein was ridiculed and dismissed as a crackpot atheist and "Bolshevik scientist." It wasn't until a total eclipse of the sun occurred in 1919 and a British expeditionary force on the island of Principe, off the coast of West Africa, was able to measure the deflection of starlight in accordance with the principles of general relativity that his theory was proved correct. Since then his theories have been measured against the physical world—from the awesome power of nuclear fission to the calculations of advanced astronomy—and found to hold. Einstein's model of the universe essentially fits.

In like manner, Buddhism has both a theoretical and a scientific basis. Nichiren revealed the law of life, Nam-myoho-renge-kyo, passing it down to his followers and future generations with an implied instruction: Here is the law, now go and test it against the realities of life and the universe. See if it works at all times, under all conditions and circumstances. All those who chant Nam-myoho-renge-kyo therefore conduct an experiment, usually an ongoing one, to determine the power and efficacy of this law in their own lives.

But, in order to have such a result, you must actually chant. You can read and talk about Buddhism, but in the end it will all be theory. The difference between purely theoretical study and Buddhist practice is like the difference between knowing mining and striking it rich. You can never know the profundity of Nam-myoho-renge-kyo until you have experienced it directly. To use another analogy, it's a little bit like explaining strawberry ice cream to a native of a remote desert kingdom who has never tasted either strawberries or ice cream. You could tell this person that it is wet and cold, creamy and sweet. But, as we all know, a verbal definition could never suffice for the actual experience of strawberry ice cream. In Buddhism as in life, there is no substitute for direct experience.

With that caution firmly in mind, let us now turn to a definition of the phrase *Nam-myoho-renge-kyo*. As we have said, this "formula" is actually based on the title of the Lotus Sutra, the pinnacle of Shakyamuni's teachings.

The title is preceded by *nam* from the Sanskrit word *namas* (to devote oneself). In Buddhism, the title of a sutra was given great weight. As Nichiren wrote, "Included within the title, or daimoku, of Nam-myoho-renge-kyo is the entire sutra consisting of all eight volumes, twenty-eight chapters, and 69,384 characters, without the omission of a single character." Like the symbols in Einstein's special theory of relativity, each of the characters in Nam-myoho-renge-kyo stands for a profound truth in life. Here they are:

Myoho means "mystic law" or that which, although true, cannot be explained. For example, what is gravity, really? Why are some people born beautiful? Or disabled? Why do some die young? Nichiren wrote:

What then does *myo* signify? It is simply the mysterious nature of our life from moment to moment, which the mind cannot comprehend or words express. When we look into our own mind at any moment, we perceive neither color nor form to verify that it exists. Yet we still cannot say it does not exist, for many differing thoughts continually occur. The mind cannot be considered either to exist or not to exist. Life is indeed an elusive reality that transcends both the words and concepts of existence and nonexistence. It is neither existence nor nonexistence, yet exhibits the qualities of both. It is the mystic entity of the Middle Way that is the ultimate reality. *Myo* is the name given to the mystic nature of life, and *ho*, to its manifestations.

As he explains, *myo* literally means "mystic," or beyond description, the ultimate reality of life, while *ho* means "all phenomena." Put together, *myoho* indicates that all phenomena of life are the expression of the law.

Nichiren also points out three meanings with regard to the character *myo*.

The first meaning is "to open," in the sense that it enables a person to develop his or her full potential as a human being. Another meaning of the character *myo* is "to revive." When its name is chanted, the mystic law has the power to revitalize one's life. The character *myo* has one additional meaning, "to be endowed with." The mystic law endows one with the fortune that protects one's happiness.

In still other writings, Nichiren describes *myo* as referring to death and *ho* to life. How can one word—*myoho* —mean so much? For one thing, written Chinese, the language of scholarship in ancient Japan and the language in which Nichiren often worked, is wonderfully descriptive, each individual character conjuring up a context of wider, related meanings. An entire book, or at least a very long chapter, could be written about *myoho*.

Next is *renge*, which literally means "lotus flower," hence the title *Lotus Sutra*. The lotus is deeply significant in the traditions of Buddhism. In nature, the lotus plant flowers and fruits at the same time, thus symbolizing the simultaneity of cause and effect.

We know from the study of the scientific method that cause and effect underlie all phenomena. Everything has its causes and its effects. The Buddha understood this more than twenty-five-hundred years ago. But in Buddhism, cause and effect have a deeper resonance as applied to human life. We create causes through thoughts, words and actions. With each cause made, an effect is registered simultaneously in the depths of life, and those effects are manifested when we meet the right environmental circumstances. The lotus flower is also symbolically prized in Buddhism because it blossoms in a muddy swamp, thereby signifying the emergence of our Buddha nature from the "swamp" of everyday desires and problems. In a similar vein, society is also likened to a muddy swamp in which we Buddhas appear. Thus, no matter how difficult our lives, how trying our circumstances, the flower of Buddhahood can always bloom.

Kyo means "sutra" or "teaching." But it can also be interpreted as "sound." The Buddha traditionally taught through the spoken word in an epoch when writing was considered unreliable and susceptible to forgery and misinterpretation. It is said that "the voice does the Buddha's work," and there is something undeniably powerful about a person chanting Nam-myoho-renge-kyo. You can sense quiet determination and strong will as the individual's rhythmic chanting fuses with the rhythm of the universe.

Taken all together then, the phrase Nam-myoho-renge-kyo could be translated as "I devote myself to the mystic law of cause and effect through sound." But it is crucial to realize that one does not need (nor is it especially desirable) to translate the phrase into English or to contemplate continuously its meaning in order to obtain benefit from chanting it. Indeed, while in the early stages of one's practice it may be difficult to understand everything, the important thing is simply to chant for one's goals with sincerity. Then, with an open mind, see what happens.

Chanting is somewhat different from conventional Western concepts of prayer. Instead of beseeching an outside force for solutions, the Buddhist musters his or her own inner resources to meet the problem. Chanting can be compared to priming a pump to bring the Buddha nature welling forth from the depths of your life. When one chants, a vow or determination is formed. Instead of "I wish such and such would happen," or "Lord, give me the strength to make such and such happen," the Buddhist's prayer is more along the lines of "I will make such and such happen" or "I vow to make the following changes in my life so that such and such happen."

Changing Your Karma

Most of us recognize the validity of cause and effect as a general rule of nature and the basis for the modern scientific method. We readily accept the notion that all causes have effects, and everything that happens in life can be traced to a series of causes, leading to a series of linked effects. You flick a light switch, the light comes on. It rains, the roof leaks. We thus tend to view the various causes and effects in linear terms as an unending chain of causes and effects. But, according to Buddhism, the reality of cause and effect is much more subtle and complex.

Buddhism teaches that cause and effect are, in essence, simultaneous. The moment a cause is created, an effect is registered like a seed planted in the depths of life. While the effect is planted the same instant the cause is created, it may not appear instantly. The effect is only manifested when the right external circumstances arise. Let's say an acorn falls to the ground and roots in the soil. It may take decades before a mighty oak tree manifests the full effect of this cause. So, while the effect may be simultaneous, in the sense that the cause for the oak tree has occurred, it is not manifested until years later. While the ultimate effect of the oak tree was latent in the acorn, it took years of rain and sunshine to achieve the right circumstances for the tree to grow. Or, to take a negative example, suppose one eats high-cholesterol foods over a period of time. It may be only after many years that the deleterious effects, arteriosclerosis and heart disease, appear. Human beings make myriad causes every day through their thoughts, words and deeds, and for each cause we receive an effect. But the effect may not be manifested for a long time.

Buddhism further subdivides the concept of cause and effect into *internal causes, external causes, latent effects* and *manifest effects.* As Daisaku Ikeda has stated:

Every activity of life occurs as the result of some external stimulus. At the same time, the true cause is the inherent cause within the human being. To give a very simple example, if someone hits you and you hit him back, the first blow is the stimulus leading to the second, but it is not the ultimate cause. You can maintain that you hit the person because he hit you, but in fact you hit him because you are you. The real cause was inside you, ready to be activated by the external cause.

To expand upon this example: Perhaps early in your life, you learned to be angry and defensive as protective responses to the behavior of others. Maybe you had a sibling who bullied you, and you learned early on that the only way to get what you wanted was to defend yourself physically, to "stand up for yourself." This internal attitude on your part, this predisposition to strike back, is what causes you to hit someone who hits you — not the mere fact of being hit. One might say that it was your karma to retaliate in such a situation.

The concept of karma, a Sanskrit word that originally meant "action," has been fundamental to Indian philosophy since the Upanishadic era, three hundred years before the awakening of Shakyamuni. There are three types of karmic action: thoughts, words and deeds. Taken together, these three types of actions, or causes, made throughout your life cumulatively form your karma. In other words, your karma is the net result of every single cause you have ever made in life (and in past lives, but more about that later). Karma can be divided broadly into good karma and bad karma, just as causes can be characterized as good causes and bad causes. These categories apply to all three forms of karmic action: thought, word and deed. For example, good karma might arise from shows of compassion and for-bearance as well as from those states of mind. Bad karma might result from such negative attitudes as greed or anger, and the various concrete actions that flow from those mental states.

Our karma is like a bank balance of latent effects we'll experience when our lives meet the right environmental conditions. Good causes produce pleasurable, beneficial effects; bad causes produce suffering. Our actions in the past exert an influence on our present existence, while our present actions shape the future.

The principle of karma, according to Nichiren, is abso-lutely precise. There is no escaping our past actions. The law of cause and effect permeates our lives throughout past, present and future existences. Nothing is forgotten, erased or missed. It is a mistake to think we can leave all our problems behind and simply move, say, to Hawaii or some other tropical paradise and live a carefree life. We carry our karma with us, like a suitcase, everywhere we go. Everything in our existence is eternally etched at the deepest levels of our lives. Have we no choice, then, but to passively accept and resign ourselves to the effects of whatever karma we forged in the past?

No. In Buddhism we create karma through our own actions and thus have the power to change. This is the promise offered by the practice of Buddhism. While, in theory, all we have to do to succeed in life is make the best possible causes, in most cases we have little control over the causes we make. We tend to be caught up in the unbroken chain of cause and effect that is our karma, for better or worse, and we act accordingly. But when we chant Nam-myoho-renge-kyo, we begin to illuminate the negative aspects of our karma—we see our own weakness vividly—and can then take steps to transform ourselves and our destiny. Nichiren used the metaphor of a mirror to suggest this process of self-perception. More than seven hundred years ago, he wrote:

> When deluded, one is called an ordinary being, but when enlightened, one is called a Buddha. This is similar to a tarnished mirror that will shine like a jewel when polished. A mind now clouded by the

illusions of the innate darkness of life is like a tarnished mirror, but when polished, it is sure to become like a clear mirror, reflecting the essential nature of phenomena and the true aspect of reality. Arouse deep faith, and diligently polish your mirror day and night. How should you polish it? Only by chanting Nam-myoho-renge-kyo.

In terms of the law of causality, Nichiren said that chanting Nam-myoho-renge-kyo was the best cause a person could make. This does not mean that a person facing a serious problem necessarily should stay home and chant all day. That is escapism. Rather, one should chant first for the wisdom to meet the problem head on, then go out and take determined action. In the clear light of enlightenment, we not only come to understand ourselves, we can also change ourselves and reach the highest imaginable plane of existence.

Ultimately, we chant Nam-myoho-renge-kyo to reveal our Buddhahood, enabling us to perceive and understand the law of the universe while, at the same time, exercising the wisdom to utilize this law. Keep in mind that, as the acorn contains the seed of a mighty oak, the seed of enlightenment is already within you. As Daisaku Ikeda has written: "When you invoke Nam-myoho-renge-kyo, you call forth your Buddha nature, or Nam-myoho-renge-kyo within you. Then you yourself are Buddha."

Road-testing Your Enlightenment

The average person, mired in the demands of everyday life, typically does not aspire to the noble and happy state of Buddhahood, at least not in any consistent way. If you have trouble paying the rent and feeding your family, it's kind of hard to walk around thinking about attaining enlightenment. So it is not unreasonable to chant for basic material and emotional needs in order to establish a firm foundation from which to aspire to higher things, including Buddhahood. The practice of Nichiren's Buddhism initially provides clear and practical benefits, foremost among them a more positive spirit—one of hopeful challenge rather than resigned defeat—that generates from deep inside. This in turn leads to wisdom and constructive action to transform whatever negative situations you may face.

To begin your practice, try chanting Nam-myoho-renge-kyo for, say, five minutes in the morning and the evening each day. Set aside the time and find a quiet place where you will not disturb others. A bedroom or den is fine. It can even be done in an automobile (but preferably not in white-knuckle commuter traffic). Sit up straight, breathe easily. Don't be disappointed if you feel a trifle bored. It is not necessary to think about anything in particular, and you do not need to contemplate the meaning of the phrase. Try to chant rhythmically.

You can chant much longer than five minutes if you wish. In times of personal crisis, when a relative or loved one is seriously ill, Buddhists will sometimes chant for hours at a time, pausing only to take a drink of water or to take care of other necessities. You can chant as often as you like and to your heart's content. But it is important to be consistent. The discipline of chanting morning and evening brings a fresh new rhythm to existence that, in and of itself, has a salutary effect.

An increased sense of hope, the improvement of a relationship, becoming more motivated—these are among the many spiritual and emotional benefits noted as people begin their Buddhist practice. In addition, beginners are often encouraged to chant for specific goals and to focus on the attainment of a clear, concrete objective. For example, if you are a salesperson, perhaps you might chant to meet your quota—or to exceed it. If you are a musician, you may want to chant to master a particularly challenging piece. These are very specific goals. On a more general plane, perhaps you wish to write poems or plays, but you have been forced to support yourself with work entirely unrelated to your dream. In this case, your goal might be to take small, incremental steps by working in your spare time to achieve your artistic goals. Through the acquisition of tangible benefits from chanting, the beginning Buddhist will find that his or her whole frame of reference changes. Those impossible dreams become very real goals.

As beginners gain experience, they find themselves not only solving their basic problems but also undergoing profound changes. Among the many results you can expect as you continue your Buddhist practice:

- *Wisdom* — the ability to derive optimum value from the knowledge one has.
- *An understanding of the eternity of life* — as we practice and observe the workings of the law of cause and effect, we begin to view life as a series of causes and effects from the past extending into the future, rather than just a moment-to-moment existence.
- *Persistence and tolerance* — the ability to challenge circumstances and cultivate the patience and stamina to work positively with the obstacles one encounters.
- *Serenity* — calmness in the face of the dynamic turbulence of life.

- *Feelings of compassion*—increased feelings of mercy and the ability to empathize with people.
- *Enlightenment*—a state permeated with wisdom, where all actions reflect one's underlying Buddha nature, a state of perfect freedom, purified of illusion and brimming with compassion.

Rome wasn't built in a day. And it is simply not possible to solve all your problems the first time you chant. A lifetime (at least) of accumulated karma, like rust, has to be carefully brushed away, day after day. But it is unusual for people who chant with some sincerity and consistency not to experience some sign or benefit—a breakthrough at work, a timely phone call from a long-lost friend, a monetary windfall, or simply the realization that they are smiling more and that others are responding to them differently. Each time we receive a benefit from chanting, we are encouraged to continue. And as we start to see actual proof of the power of our Buddhist practice, we naturally come to share our experiences with others. This sharing with other people is another key to developing our inner potential for enlightenment, or Buddhahood. Eventually we will find ourselves chanting enthusiastically for the happiness of friends, family and coworkers. For it is integral to the process of becoming

enlightened to realize that the individual self is connected to all other people, and that our happiness is
linked to the overall happiness of the society in which we
live.

As the poet John Donne wrote, "No man is an Island."
In the depths of life, we are all part of the same cosmic
life force. Therefore, it is essential that we practice for
the sake of ourselves and for others. As we shall see in
the next chapter, Buddhism teaches that our own lives
are intricately linked to our friends, our physical environment, our world—even the universe itself.

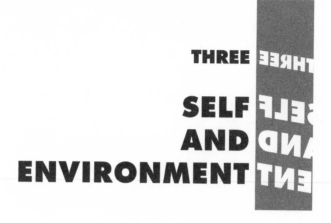

THREE

SELF
AND
ENVIRONMENT

If you wish to change society,
change yourself first.
—Thomas Carlyle

A great human revolution in just a single
individual will help achieve a change
in the destiny of all humankind.
—Daisaku Ikeda

IN A CLASSIC SEQUENCE from the movie *Singin' in the Rain*, Gene Kelly dances down a studio-lot city street amidst a driving downpour, kicking up his heels and twirling athletically around lampposts, joyous despite the wet weather. This film has been beloved by people of all ages for decades, and not just because it cheers us up. It also points to an underlying truth often ignored in the day-to-day reality of life: Although the outside world can be sunny or cloudy, what really matters is how we feel inside.

An enlightened person is one who can face a hurricane of obstacles with wisdom and poise. This image of inward contentment amid outward turmoil is a perfect one to introduce the Buddhist concept of the oneness of subject and environment.

As a practical matter, we tend to think of our skin as defining the boundary between our bodies and the outside

world. We view the interaction between these two separate realms as limited to ingestion, respiration and the
occasional pinpricks of reality. But in Buddhist philosophy, our lives are seen as an inextricable part of our physical environment, united at their very depths with other
people and with the great cosmic life force of the universe.

Let's use a very basic example to show how this grand
idea might have some validity. It is common knowledge
that the earth's gravitational force acts upon all living
things. Now suppose you bounce a ball high into the air.
The trajectory of the ball is influenced by various mech-
anisms operating within the ball itself (density of the
rubber, etc.), the strength of your arm and the earth's
gravitational resistance. But what is probably less obvious is that the ball's flight is also subtly influenced by
other cosmological objects in the universe. Not just the
earth but also the moon, the sun and the stars are acting upon the ball. These celestial bodies' remote influence is like a message from the outer bounds of the
cosmos. That a celestial body light-years from earth is
influencing life here is amazing. But it is true. To take an
example closer to home (a mere 93 million miles away):
If the surface temperature of our own star, the sun, were
to rise even a few degrees, the effects would be cata-

strophic here on earth, from melting polar ice that would change our weather to deadly ultraviolet rays that would force everyone to live indoors.

Interwoven throughout the so-called outside world are innumerable invisible threads that link the individual to the macrocosm. The percentage of ions in the air, even the color of a room, can subtly affect our emotions. Our own behavior exerts an undeniable impact on the people around us. And human society has an undeniable impact on the natural environment. We are not separate from the world we live in, but involved in a dynamic interaction with it. Buddhism goes even further. According to the life philosophy expounded by Shakyamuni, illuminated by T'ien-t'ai, and perfected by Nichiren in thirteenth-century Japan, one's environment and circumstances actually mirror one's inner life. All of these thinkers realized that the world cannot be divorced from our perception of it. In this they anticipated the work of twentieth-century physicists like Albert Einstein, Niels Bohr and Werner Heisenberg. Who you are greatly determines the quality of your surroundings. It is not a very easy concept to accept, because it goes against our ingrained prejudice to blame circumstances for our problems. It is especially difficult to live by, since in the West we have largely succeeded in subduing our environment and achieving a high level of material well-being by viewing the self and nature as essentially separate.

In Buddhism, however, this inseparability of the person and his or her surroundings is an all-embracing vision of reality. As Nichiren wrote in a letter to a follower:

> The essence of the sutras preached before the Lotus Sutra is that all phenomena arise from the mind. To illustrate, they say that the mind is like the great earth, while the grasses and trees are like all phenomena. But it is not so with the Lotus Sutra. It teaches that the mind itself is the great earth, and that the great earth itself is the grasses and trees.

This does not mean that life is a dream. Rather, it suggests that there is no fundamental difference between mind and matter.

If we were to apply these notions to the realm of human relations, certain insights would emerge. We would begin to realize that the lives of those in our immediate environment tend to mirror our own inner lives. Generally, if an individual finds other people unfriendly, it is often because he or she is provoking that reaction, one way or another. Similarly, if that person becomes friendlier, the people around that person will begin to react differently. An unusually kind and good-hearted person will tend to believe that others are the same. To a person possessed by lust for power, even the most selfless, benevolent actions of others will appear as cunning moves to gain power. When we cherish people with the same profound reverence as we would the Buddha, their Buddha nature functions to protect us. On the other hand, if we belittle or regard people with contempt, we will be disparaged in return, as though gazing into our own image reflected in a mirror. As much as we sometimes resist the idea, a smile and a few kind words can achieve near miracles by reducing hostility in many situations. There are people who can walk into a room and immediately lighten things up and lift everyone's spirits. These are all illustrations of what Buddhism terms the principle of the oneness of life and its environment.

The Oneness of Life and Environment

The principle of the oneness of life (or subject) and environment is worth examining at some length. The Japanese term for this principle is *esho funi*. The first word is a contraction of *eho* (environment) and *shoho* (subject or self). The second word, *funi*, indicates "two but not two." Life and its environment, or, in other words, sentient and insentient things, are frequently considered to be separate entities ("two"). This is how they appear to us, and this is how we regard them. But on another level, they are "not two." Research in the natural sciences has revealed the complex interaction of living organisms and their surroundings. The chain of cause and effect surrounding even simple phenomena—a raindrop falling on one's cheek—can be astoundingly intricate. Weather, ecology and the brain are examples of complex systems that cannot be fully understood by mathematical analysis or simulations. Why is it that science cannot adequately account for such natural occurrences? One reason is that in such phenomena, very small, imperceptible events can produce very great changes—the so-called butterfly effect.

The butterfly effect gets its name from the following scenario: Suppose a butterfly deep in the Amazon rain forest flaps its wings. The tiny action then becomes the starting point for a seemingly infinite chain of events— a leaf falls from a branch, a ripple moves across a pond, a wave causes the wind to stir—eventually resulting in a change in the weather in some faraway corner of the earth. But though the same butterfly may flap its wings the next day, it might have no effect on the weather at all. This uncertainty is one of the distinctive aspects of the "science of complexity," which in recent years has arisen as a challenge to analytical science.

The butterfly effect can also be extended to the interpersonal sphere by using a little imagination. The raised eyebrow or the quick rolling of one's eyes in a business meeting can have, if observed by the wrong person, wide-ranging consequences for one's career. The subtlest gesture made in the presence of a lover—perhaps the merest sigh or a barely perceptible shrug of impatience—can change the course of a relationship.

As the increasingly sophisticated measurements and methods of modern science reveal the subtle links between seemingly disparate events in nature, and thus the interconnectedness of all things, our view of the world is changing. Indeed, the age-old Buddhist concept of self and environment as "two but not two" is gradually becoming accepted in the Western world. As the late English historian Arnold Toynbee said in a published dialogue with Daisaku Ikeda:

The mental distinction between a living being and its environment would, I think, be found to have no counterpart in reality.... *Esho funi* seems to be a concise explanation of what I suppose the true condition is. A living being's egoistic attempt to organize the universe around itself is the condition for, and the expression of, its vitality.... Altruism, alias love, is an attempt to reverse the natural effort of a living being to organize the universe round itself. Love is a counterattempt, on the living being's part, to devote itself to the universe instead of exploiting the universe.

No one exists in isolation. We are connected to parents who conceived and raised us, to teachers who have educated us, and to friends who have encouraged us. We are also linked to people we have never met who harvest and distribute our food, manufacture our clothing, write the books that shape our thinking—in fact, we are connected to everyone whose efforts help hold together the fabric of society. There is no one in the world who has no connection to us. The playwright John Guare dramatized this notion in *Six Degrees of Separation*, in which a character theorizes that every person can be linked to every other person on the planet by tracing his or her relationships through no more than six other people. Our "self" encompasses all other people. Viewed from a deeper perspective, everyone is linked to everyone else by virtue of the fact that all participate in the same ultimate reality of life, the Buddha nature.

Although the inner world of self and the external world of reality appear to be distinct, ultimately they are not two, but one — not just closely interconnected or mutually dependent, but inseparable from one another. In Buddhism, we call this oneness "the true aspect of all phenomena," the ultimate truth, or the Buddha nature. Nichiren also called it the Mystic Law, which he expressed as Nam-myoho-renge-kyo. The relationship between the self and the ultimate truth is termed "mystic" because it is beyond our intellectual comprehension. But that doesn't mean we can't think about it, discuss it, and test its value in our lives. Furthermore, even though it is mystic, let's not lose sight of the fact that it frames a view of humanity and universe that is increasingly confirmed by science.

Freedom From the Sufferings of Birth and Death

Read the following excerpt from one of Nichiren's most famous letters, titled "On Attaining Buddhahood in This Lifetime," written during what would have been the

Middle Ages in the West (1255), and see if it doesn't strike you as somehow modern:

> If you wish to free yourself from the sufferings of birth and death you have endured since time without beginning and to attain without fail unsurpassed enlightenment in this lifetime, you must perceive the mystic truth that is originally inherent in all living beings. This truth is Myoho-renge-kyo. Chanting Myoho-renge-kyo [see editor's note that follows] will therefore enable you to grasp the mystic truth innate in all life.
>
> The Lotus Sutra is the king of sutras, true and correct in both word and principle. Its words are the ultimate reality, and this reality is the Mystic Law (*myoho*). It is called the Mystic Law because it reveals the principle of the mutually inclusive relationship of a single moment of life and all phenomena. That is why this sutra is the wisdom of all Buddhas.
>
> Life at each moment encompasses the body and mind and the self and environment of all sentient beings in the Ten Worlds as well as all insentient beings in the three thousand realms, including plants, sky, earth, and even the minutest particles

of dust. Life at each moment permeates the entire realm of phenomena and is revealed in all phenomena. To be awakened to this principle is itself the mutually inclusive relationship of life at each moment and all phenomena. Nevertheless, even though you chant and believe in Myoho-renge-kyo, if you think the Law is outside yourself, you are embracing not the Mystic Law but an inferior teaching.... Therefore, when you chant...you must summon up deep faith that Myoho-renge-kyo is your life itself.

[Editor's Note: Here Nichiren chooses to omit the character *Nam,* meaning "devotion to," in favor of the literal title of the Lotus Sutra, *Myoho-renge-kyo.* However, the letter concludes with the phrase Nam-myoho-renge-kyo, written twice, to indicate that this is the correct invocation.]

For Nichiren, "freedom from the sufferings of birth and death," meant to transcend the laws of decay and decline, defined earlier as the theory of insubstantiality. Nothing lasts forever. The solidity, the substance of life, is an illusion. Particle physics teaches us that at the subatomic level we cannot speak of fixed or solid matter but only of constantly shifting energy patterns or waves. As physicists tell us, matter is composed not simply of atoms, with their seemingly discrete electrons, protons and neutrons, but of even smaller, more mysterious units of darting matter and energy called leptons, quarks, bosons, weak forces and dark forces. The world of quantum mechanics is so unstable and elusive that no matter how hard they try, physicists find it difficult to pin down the primary building blocks. To do so would require some fixed reference point, and that is exactly what reality, at the subatomic level, refuses to provide. The philosopher of science Jacob Bronowski wrote in *The Ascent of Man*:

> The quip among professors was...that on Mondays, Wednesdays, and Fridays the electron would behave like a particle; on Tuesdays, Thursdays, and Saturdays it would behave like a wave. How could you match those two aspects, brought from the large-scale world and pushed into a single entity, into this Lilliput, *Guillver's Travels* world of the inside of the atom?

Now let us return to the words of Nichiren: *you must summon up deep faith that Myoho-renge-kyo is your life itself.* "Your life itself" could be interpreted as the very stuff we are made of—the "waves" between the particles, the vibration that characterizes the particles, the energy in the interstices between them, the particles themselves, such as they are. Nichiren thus, in addition to giving us marvelous insight into what to think about while chanting, is advising us that this sound we are making when we chant Nam-myoho-renge-kyo is, in truth, the rhythm of the universe. When we chant we are vibrating to that universal tune, that underlying harmony that is a part of all things.

As we have seen, Buddhism, like physics, teaches that everything is in constant flux. But it has a very different aim in doing so. Rather than actively striving to clarify the nature of the physical world (which it does in passing), Buddhism seeks to illuminate the human condition. To Nichiren, "freedom" meant not an escape from the realm of changing phenomena but the discovery of an absolute point of reliance within ourselves. This liberates us from the bonds of karma as a result of manifesting Buddha wisdom to perceive the true nature of all phenomena, including our relationship with them.

Because individual and surroundings are fundamentally one, whatever state of life we manifest will simultaneously manifest in the environment. That is what Nichiren meant when he wrote, at another time, "Environment is like the shadow, and life, the body." If the body wavers, the environment does, too. If the body shows respect, the environment respects in return. A person whose basic life tendency is hatred and hostility will bring forth anguish and misery in his or her surroundings, while someone with the basic state of Buddhahood will enjoy protection and support from the world. When Nichiren stated that you should not "think the Law is outside yourself," he meant not to seek the source and solutions to one's sufferings in the environment. To compare ourselves continually with others, whether we evaluate ourselves negatively or positively, or to think that other people should be responsible for our happiness, or that we cannot be happy until someone else changes, or that our bank balance must increase in order for us to feel self-worth—these are all examples of seeking the Law outside ourselves. Like the early American transcendental philosophy of Emerson and Thoreau, Buddhist thinking has a strong core of self-reliance.

The Power of Taking Responsibility

If our environment truly mirrors our lives (and it does), is everything then our fault? And isn't this simply blaming the victim?

The fact is, as Buddhism acknowledges, problems are natural. To be alive is to face problems—the problem of feeding ourselves and the pangs of suffering when we go hungry, the problem of living safely in a violent society, the problem of raising children to be happy and self-actualized. And many, many more. Such problems are not our fault, they are simply part of what it means to be alive.

Also, while we are not responsible for the behavior of others—that's their responsibility—we do need to be responsible for our own behavior. This includes taking responsibility for being in the circumstances we find ourselves in, no matter how difficult and arbitrary such circumstances might seem.

It may not be clear at first what causes led to being poor or hard of hearing or incredibly shy. Yet Buddhism explains that, when viewed from the perspective of the eternity of life and the myriad of good and bad causes we have made, we did, in fact, make the causes to be where and who we are in this life. It is entirely the result of our own actions over many lifetimes. All of us are ultimately responsible for everything about our lives.

We really are the architects of our existence, and our surroundings do reflect precisely what we have built. Buddhism entails a radical sense of responsibility and empowers the individual to effect change. If we are unhappy in our circumstances, we have the ability to do something about them.

The idea of taking responsibility for our own lives has become a voguish one in American society, probably because so many of us, especially those in public life, have shirked the notion for so long. But the kind of responsibility we're talking about here is, well, rather extreme. The Buddhist view of life asks us to accept 100 percent responsibility for our lives.

It might be difficult to imagine being held responsible for something like having a terrible boss. But, didn't you choose your job and haven't you chosen to stay at the company throughout this period? You didn't make your boss a bad one. It's not your fault that the boss is bad. You are responsible, however, for being and staying there. Also, most bosses, no matter how demanding and arrogant, usually have a stable of favorites, employees who do their bidding and get along with them fairly smoothly. Why aren't you one of these people? Have you chosen not to be, out of high-mindedness or some other motive? Whatever the reason, it was your choice. In fact, the more closely we examine any situation in life, using the Buddhistic eye of clarity and wisdom, the more we will realize that we are indeed responsible for all our choices and thus for our experience with our environment, for better or worse.

Yet, you may still think this discussion is downright

absurd. How can the individual be held responsible for, say, an earthquake? Or a plane crash?

Paradigms of this kind of thinking seldom can be found from outside the Buddhist world, but sometimes they do. Take the Academy Award-winning movie *Rain Man*. In that film, you may recall, the character played by Dustin Hoffman, the shuffling, mumbling Raymond (his younger brother could not properly pronounce his name, hence "Rain Man") is severely autistic. He has spent most of his life in a mental institution yet has an uncanny gift for mathematics. When his younger brother, Charlie, played by the actor Tom Cruise, tries to get him to California within a limited time frame, complications develop. At one point, they are in an airport and Charlie is trying to choose a flight to Los Angeles. After settling on one, an American Airlines flight, Raymond demurs. Why? Because American has had several fatal air accidents in the past several decades. In frustration, Charlie suggests Continental Airlines. Again, Raymond digs into his memory bank and spews a series of numbers detailing the passengers killed or injured in Continental crashes. Finally, Charlie throws up his hands in frustration and asks, what airline will you fly on?

"Qantas" is the answer.

Qantas, the Australian national airline, has never been

involved in a fatal crash. Of course, Qantas doesn't fly domestically in the United States, so it is not an option. They end up renting a car.

Underlying the comic absurdity of the scene is a potent point: When you fly, you must take responsibility for the chance, albeit a very small chance, that the plane will go down. Anyone who flies on a commercial airline is taking a certain risk. It is a small risk, much smaller statistically than driving an automobile. But the risk is there. Buddhism does not blame you for being aboard a jet when it crashes. But it does require you to take responsibility. After all, it was your choice to take that flight and board that plane, or even to fly at all.

Surely no one can be blamed for being caught in an earthquake. But the question may reasonably be asked: Were you aware of the seismic history of the place where you lived or were visiting? People who live near the San Andreas Fault (the populations of Los Angeles and San Francisco, for example) should be aware that they have some responsibility for settling in one of the world's most notoriously unstable areas, just as people who build their homes on a flood plain have to live with the risk of being flooded during severe storm seasons.

There are no accidents in life, according to Buddhism,

and there are no coincidences. There is only the iron law of cause and effect or, to put it more precisely, Nam-myoho-renge-kyo. When you adopt the Buddhist view, when you deeply internalize this law within your life, you begin to gain tremendous power over yourself—and over your relationship with the world outside.

The Object for Attaining Buddhahood

The question now might be reasonably asked: This theoretical stuff is all well and good, but how I am supposed to translate it into my everyday life? It certainly is not enough merely to look at the world differently from time to time, or to make some cool, intellectual decision that the oneness of subject and environment is the correct way of thinking. In the Buddhism we are discussing, "right thinking" without diligent practice becomes, in the end, just idealism. It will not change one's life. Fortunately, even though the theory behind chanting Nam-myoho-renge-kyo is profound, the basic practice itself is easy. Whether or not you understand what Nam-myoho-renge-kyo means, or "the mutually inclusive relationship of life and all phenomena," or any other terms in this book, you can still achieve great benefits by chanting this single phrase, just as you can boot up your computer by pushing a button, although you may have no real idea how it works.

The aim of Buddhist practice is not to "understand" the truth as an object external to ourselves but to become one with the truth. In Buddhist technical terminology, this is called the fusion of reality or object and wisdom or subject. As we have pointed out, traditional Buddhist meditation aims to transcend the subject–object barrier and realize the perfect oneness of the self and external reality. Concerning this principle, Nichiren wrote:

> Is not the meaning of the sutra and the commentary that the way to Buddhahood lies within the two elements of reality and wisdom? Reality means the true nature of all phenomena, and wisdom means the illuminating and manifesting of this true nature. Thus when the riverbed of reality is infinitely broad and deep, the water of wisdom will flow ceaselessly. When this reality and wisdom are fused, one attains Buddhahood in one's present form.

The Buddha realizes the perfect identity of oneself and the Law, or ultimate reality. It sounds elementary, especially if one believes, intellectually, in the essential oneness of humans and their universe, as described above. We are all Buddhas, after all, right? The fact that we have the Buddha nature inherent within us, however, does not in itself mean that we are actually Buddhas. We only awaken to this Buddha nature when our subjective wisdom completely fuses with objective reality. To make this possible for all, Nichiren embodied his own enlightenment in an object of devotion called the Gohonzon, a scroll with the words Nam-myoho-renge-kyo written down the center in bold characters.

Today, the Gohonzon corresponds to the object, while our practice to the Gohonzon corresponds to the subject, or subjective wisdom. When we chant Nam-myoho-renge-kyo to the Gohonzon, the subject–object dichotomy dissolves, enabling us to fuse with the macrocosm. In that moment, we manifest the state of Buddhahood.

How is this fusion accomplished? The term *nam* of Nam-myoho-renge-kyo indicates "devotion" or our practice of chanting to the Gohonzon. Through our daily practice we devote our lives to or fuse our lives with the ultimate, unchanging reality embodied in the Gohonzon. As a result of our efforts we simultaneously draw forth an infinite wisdom that functions in accordance with our changing circumstances. This latter is the wisdom through which we human beings can experience boundless joy and freedom despite the uncertainties of our daily lives.

After you have chanted, for example, people may capture your attention in fresh new ways. Complex relationships seem clearer, perhaps for the first time. When you go to your office, the Byzantine politics and backstage intrigues emerge into focus. Hey, you suddenly realize, beneath all his bravado and arbitrary behavior, the boss is actually an insecure person who wants to be liked. At home, long-standing emotional logjams also yield to supple new insights. All of these subtle new perceptions stem from seeing the world with the eye of wisdom. The gulf that typically exists between objective reality and your subjective wisdom has been bridged. For most of us, the problems of life stem from the large discrepancy between reality and our subjective assessment of it. Now, perhaps for the first time in a long time, you can use this wisdom, this incredible overview of complex situations, to supply the compassionate action needed to solve problems.

Practice for Self and Others

Since our lives are inseparable from the life of the universe, and since we as individuals are connected to everyone else on earth, then we must also take responsibility for the happiness of our loved ones and friends.

As the saying goes, if your neighbor's house is burning, can you really be safe? This realization gives rise to what Buddhism calls the way of the bodhisattva. A bodhisattva is one who strives for enlightenment while at the same time working to help others attain the same goal. In practical terms, efforts made for the sake of others actually do more to help change one's own karma than efforts made purely to transform oneself. Practice for others may include sharing one's experience, providing moral and emotional support and instilling hope, and, ultimately, helping others to practice Buddhism. Yes, Buddhism is highly individualistic, based primarily on one's solitary efforts in chanting. But if one's efforts are directed only toward self-improvement, any truth obtained will be only partial.

Here then is a paradox in Buddhism. While we say that the primary practice for growth is the individual chanting to the Gohonzon, there is no true revolution of the self without extending ourselves toward others. Robert Thurman, author and professor of religion at Columbia University, once conducted an entire workshop based on a simple precept recorded by Shantideva, an eighth-century Indian monk, "All the happiness in the world comes from thinking of others; all the suffering in the world comes from thinking of only oneself." By concerning yourself with the problems of others, your own problems become diminished, both in perspective, because you realize that perhaps other people have more serious obstacles than yours, and in reality, because when you stop focusing on your own difficulties they lose their mastery over you.

It is said that a drop of ink in a cup of water will turn the water blue. This same drop in the ocean will vanish completely. Likewise, by immersing ourselves in the life struggles of other people, as we develop our natural capacity for compassion (what Buddhism calls our bodhisattva nature), we gain the wisdom and life force to overcome our own problems.

Life is a moment-to-moment battle between one's Buddha nature and the workings of delusion. When we chant Nam-myoho-renge-kyo and reach out to others, we can tap our Buddha nature and overcome our deluded nature. This principle also can be applied to society: When the humanistic ideals of Buddhism spread, society will become more humane in every aspect. According to the principle of the oneness of life and its environment, the environment reflects both the positive and the negative. Therefore, from the problem of war to the ongoing threats to the global ecosystem, real lasting change depends on bringing forth the enlightened nature of uncountable individuals. Establishing within our lives and within society the humane philosophy that Buddhism puts forth is an effective way to bring peace and harmony to our world.

FOUR

HAPPINESS

We hold these truths to be self-evident,
that all men are created equal, that they
are endowed by their Creator with certain
unalienable Rights, that among these are Life,
Liberty and the pursuit of Happiness.
— Thomas Jefferson
(from the Declaration of Independence)

Most people are about as happy
as they make up their minds to be.
— Abraham Lincoln

BUDDHISM teaches that happiness is the purpose of life. It is not, however, something that happens without effort. Since obstacles continually turn up as we make our way through life, many of us never fully realize this most fundamental of life's aims, except for brief interludes. Often our experience of happiness is so fleeting that we obsessively hark back to "the good times" and generally feel restless and unsatisfied the rest of the time. "We were happy when we were young," is a common refrain (in reality, when we really were young, we were anxious and awkward, had bad skin and a host of other problems). Or, "We were truly happy on that summer vacation" (when, in truth, we were bored and badly sunburned). Or, "I was happy when I was with Mary" (although there were sufficient reasons for you to leave Mary or for Mary to leave you). And so on. And on. Something happened, things changed and along with the change went our happiness.

Through correct Buddhist practice, one can create the fundamental causes that lead to indestructible happiness. The teachings of Buddhism explain the "secret" that makes it possible to enjoy life fully—not just to *pursue* happiness interminably but to actually catch and hold on to it right here, right now, just as you are. But first, it is necessary to define happiness so that we know exactly what we are seeking.

Ever since Jefferson, Americans have believed firmly in their right to the "pursuit of Happiness." When compared with other things that people hope for—health, wealth, success, status—happiness is rated highest for most of us. Along with life and liberty, without which it is largely an irrelevant consideration, happiness is at the very foundation of the American way of life.

It is worth pointing out, however, that Jefferson's famous *pursuit of Happiness* is thought by many scholars to denote free enterprise—that is, the ability of individuals to pursue their economic destiny unfettered by foreign regulation and burdensome taxes. It was part of the new worldview of the period that if people were left alone to pursue their economic ambitions—something that had been denied to the colonists in Europe—this liberated condition would constitute happiness. Today, amid material comfort and affluence undreamed of in

Jefferson's time, we know this definition to be incomplete. Mighty capitalists and builders of great personal fortunes are not necessarily happy persons.

Nevertheless, life, liberty and the *purchase* of happiness have increasingly become the new American ideals. While it is undeniably enjoyable to purchase the "toys" we believe will make us happy, it is also true that the joy we feel is not long lasting. The new-car excitement quickly fades amid the reality of continued car payments. New clothes wear out or go out of style. To recreate the joy of the initial purchase, we buy more and more, again and again. No surprise then that the belief that we would be happier if we just had more money has become conventional wisdom.

Myths About Happiness

The predominant view of happiness in America suggests that—in addition to wealth—fame, success, youth and beauty are critical components of being happy. After all aren't the young, rich, famous and good-looking happier? Doesn't the one who collects the most toys win the game of life?

Psychologists and researchers who have long focused on analyzing the causes of unhappiness—depression, stress, grief—are beginning to focus their attention on happiness.

Their conclusion: Happiness is not what most people suppose it to be.

Astonishingly, they have found repeatedly that differences among people that we take as significant indicators of happiness (such as money, age, gender, health, race, education, employment and geography) have minimal effects on overall satisfaction in life. Startling as it may seem, circumstances have little to do with happiness.

Compounding the problem is the tendency to compare ourselves with others against these illusory standards, increasing the sense of restless dissatisfaction that fuels unhappiness. We strive to keep up with others because they appear to be happier than we are. It turns out that in all the usual areas of comparison, they probably aren't.

The problem is, we believe them to be. And it is this misperception that creates real unhappiness where none existed before. Advertisers exploit our willingness to compare ourselves with the images of others who appear to be better off (and consequently happier) than us. Bombarding us with images of people whose elegant possessions (extravagant lifestyles, gorgeous bodies, harmonious families, etc.) awaken our envy, they enlarge our circle of comparisons and whet our appetites for what others have. This manufactured unhappiness is used as a motivator to get us to purchase the "missing" ingredient of our happiness.

It is also widely believed that we would be happier if we had fewer problems or that once the problem we are immediately facing is resolved, happiness will result. But it never quite happens that way. Today's problem is replaced by new problems in an unending procession. We seem barely to have a chance to catch our breath before new challenges confront us. This way of thinking equates problems with unhappiness. Is it possible to establish a problem-free life for any significant length of time? Buddhism says no.

Sustainable happiness is not the absence of problems. As Nichiren writes: "Though worldly troubles may arise, never let them disturb you. No one can avoid problems, not even sages or worthies." Everybody has problems. Yet we all know people with enormous problems who are happy and people with every advantage who are miserable.

Buddhism describes life in terms of an accumulation of sufferings arising within the eternal cycle of birth, aging, sickness and death. There are other kinds of sufferings, certainly, including losing a loved one, depression,

being fired from a job, living in poverty within an afflu-
ent society, experiencing the barriers of race and ethnic-
ity—all of which add to suffering and anguish.

At the most fundamental level, Buddhism recognizes
that life is filled with problems. This existential outlook
has begun to percolate through Western culture. "Life is
difficult," are the opening words of M. Scott Peck's *The
Road Less Traveled*, one of the most popular self-help
books ever written. "This is a great truth, one of the
greatest truths," Peck writes and, in a footnote, explains
that this is the first of the Four Noble Truths taught by
the Buddha.

To understand that life means difficulty liberates us
because it helps us to understand problems and suffering as natural parts of life, not as signs of our inadequa-
cies. There is a saying, "A small heart gets used to misery
and becomes docile, while a great heart towers above
misfortune." From the Buddhist perspective, the fact
that life is filled with problems is no reason to be
depressed, downhearted or resigned to a miserable fate.
Buddhism is not Stoicism.

Buddhism finds happiness in the midst of rather than
the absence of problems.

The reason so many people are unhappy is, for the
most part, delusion. They believe the predominant

myths that our culture propagates about happiness.

Nichiren explained that the only difference between a Buddha (a person who has attained true happiness) and a common mortal (a person who has not) is that the common mortal is deluded while the Buddha is enlightened. Simply stated, human beings fail to understand the true nature of happiness. As a result they are often unable to find it because they are looking in the wrong places.

To meet our realistic expectations of achieving happiness takes more than effort. We must know what happiness is, what it is not, and, most important, have a practical method for getting it. Nichiren elucidated the practice that enables us to accomplish the construction of lasting indestructible happiness.

Relative vs. Absolute Happiness

According to the Mahayana Buddhism taught by Nichiren, there are two types of happiness: relative (temporary) and absolute (lasting).

Relative happiness is the feeling of satisfaction, gratification or elation experienced from achieving some goal or having our desires fulfilled. Because of the temporal nature of what we achieve or acquire, this kind of happiness usually wanes over time. If we are fundamentally unhappy individuals, we remain so, often becoming more despondent than ever after experiencing joy, because we feel its absence so keenly.

For example, if you have been happily married, the death of a spouse can plunge you into the depths of misery. Also, there are many who reach the end of their lives lonely, destitute and miserable despite having gained some degree of fame or popularity.

Neither wealth, status, fame nor beauty can assure us of a happy life. This is because happiness based on these things is relative happiness. It is dependent, circumstantial and temporary. Whoever strives to construct a happy life based on wealth, status, fame or beauty will eventually encounter dissatisfaction, loss and unhappiness. Instead, Buddhism expounds a happiness that is absolute and lasting. Absolute happiness is a state of life in which we can enjoy our existence under any circumstances. The state of absolute happiness is also called Buddhahood.

We are born in this life to be happy, not merely to endure suffering. This is a basic premise of the Buddhism taught by Nichiren and the Soka Gakkai International, the lay organization of Nichiren followers throughout the world.

How can we attain lasting happiness when our usual state of being is so mercurial?

A core Buddhist principle called the Ten Worlds systematically outlines the ceaseless moment-to-moment drama of our inner lives. This principle teaches that we are continually experiencing varying states of being that operate at a level far below the conscious mind. These states, from lowest to highest, are:

1) Hell
2) Hunger
3) Animality
4) Anger
5) Humanity
6) Heaven (Rapture; it is also referred to as relative or temporary happiness)
7) Learning
8) Realization
9) Bodhisattva (compassion)
10) Buddhahood (also called enlightenment or absolute happiness).

Nearly everyone has a tendency to dwell in one world more than in the others. For example, from an early age one might have become well known for having a short fuse in dealing with others. People with such a temper tend to occupy the world of Anger. Or maybe you tend to be a passive, timid sort, who lets the chips fall where they may. Perhaps Humanity is your dominant world and passivity your Achilles' heel. Maybe you are one who can never get enough, whether it be money or sex or approval. Hunger, then, is your world. We could call this one's "life tendency" or, better yet, one's karma. Most of us struggle through life with the same, unchanging tendency dominating our professional, social and family interactions. Try as we might, there are always one or two worlds, or life-conditions, that we seem to gravitate toward. Despite even Herculean efforts at self-improvement, we often find it extremely difficult to change this fundamental tendency.

To illustrate how these Ten Worlds, or conditions of life, might function within your own psyche, let's imagine an ordinary "day in the life...."

You wake up, get out of bed, perhaps even drag a comb across your head, as in the Beatles song. You have your morning coffee. You read the paper. Perhaps you have a Labrador dozing peacefully at your feet. You are in the world of Humanity (5), where one remains in neutral gear.

Now you head out into the world, begin your daily commute and get into bumper-to-bumper traffic. Immediately you are cut off and nearly hit by someone vying for incremental advantage. You exchange hostile glances with this inconsiderate person. For a flashing instant, you are in the world of Anger (4).

Arriving at work, you find that your immediate superior has again taken credit for your best work and, again, piled your desk with boring, low-profile assignments. Disgusted but lacking the courage to confront authority, you instead snap at your assistant and begin doling out as many unpleasant tasks to him as you can find. You have sunk into the world of Animality (3), where one is easily dominated and, in turn, seeks to dominate others.

The day wears on and you go to lunch. As usual, you can't help noticing individuals you find attractive. Alas, you are not currently seeing anyone — in fact, you have almost given up the hope of ever meeting the right person. Indeed, this woeful, resigned feeling colors everything you see and do. You are in the world of Hunger (2), where strong, unfulfilled desires distort your view of reality.

Returning to your office, you call a recent flame and ask for a date. This person tells you, however, that the relationship is really over, that you have personal tastes, including your love of modern jazz, that make further contact impossible. Shocked and hurt, you begin to feel that you will never be happy, that there is no way out.

Your career is a dud. You can't sustain a relationship. Your problems are overwhelming. You are now in the world of Hell (1), a condition of utmost suffering, where even the possibility of achieving some degree of happiness seems impossible.

Just at this moment, when all hope seems lost, the telephone rings. It is a professional acquaintance, a very attractive one, calling with an extra ticket to a jazz concert that night. Would you care to come? Instantly, you are in Heaven (6), the world where desires have been fulfilled—a state of *relative* happiness (sometimes also called Rapture). Your entire attitude toward the day has changed. The circumstances that put you in Hell shrink in magnitude, and an aura of good fortune suffuses your life. (In Buddhism, Heaven and Hell are not places but conditions of life.)

Such is the shifting interior landscape of human existence. Perhaps you can even recognize the variability of your own mind in the flow of thought and emotion that occurs in this story. Our inner lives are kaleidoscopic, changing color and pattern with infinite variety and subtlety amid the welter and chaos of contemporary existence. In truth, when something happens to elate us, our fundamental circumstances have hardly changed at all; what has changed is the person within, and that person has been constantly changing from the moment the alarm rang.

The worlds we have described so far are known in Buddhism as the "six paths" or "six lower worlds." For the vast majority of the human race, life is primarily a matter of bouncing back and forth, as in a pinball machine, among these six worlds. One might reasonably ask: What's wrong with being in the worlds of Humanity and Heaven?

The problem is that these states don't last. In the lower six paths, we are living primarily in reaction to external circumstances. In these lower worlds, we are at the mercy of our environment. Our well-being is contingent on something or someone else. A person in the lower worlds is thus doomed to a roller-coaster existence —happy when things go well, unhappy when things don't—ultimately experiencing little control in life in spite of often prodigious effort. True happiness can never be rooted in this shifting quicksand.

But within us exists the potential for a different, more solid kind of happiness, culminating in the absolute happiness of Buddhahood. The higher worlds, including Buddhahood, are known as the "four noble worlds."

Unlike the conditional, reactive states of the lower six, the first three noble worlds of Learning, Realization and

Bodhisattva are proactive, not reactive, states. The Buddhism of Nichiren uses these states as the basis for a practice that leads us to the self-created state of absolute happiness.

Let us now return to our "day in the life" scenario. Buoyed by the phone call and wishing to avoid sinking into a morass of negative feelings about your job, you plunge with renewed enthusiasm into your work, a major research project you have been involved in for some time, a project that heightens your understanding of your profession and the way the world works. The hours fly by like minutes. You are in the world of Learning (7), where you gain knowledge about life, even if it is entirely within a non-Buddhist framework. Returning home, you decide to play the piano for a bit to pass the time before your date. You find yourself increasingly absorbed in a particular jazz riff, which you explore through myriad variations. You are now in the eighth world, Realization, typically described as a kind of awakening that comes through discipline. It is also characterized as the thrill of mastering a difficult skill, and it applies as much to building a boat in the backyard or learning needlepoint as it does to writing a sonnet or a symphony.

Now let us suppose that a soulful piano chord prompts you to remember a sick friend in the hospital. You decide to visit her on the way to the jazz concert. You are now in the world of Bodhisattva (9), or compassion, characterized by a willingness to help others. This world is also known as "aspiration for enlightenment," since, as we shall see, concern for the happiness and well-being of others is integral to the conduct of a Buddha.

Buddhahood: What Happiness Is

The tenth and highest world is more difficult to describe because we don't often experience it. Nichiren talks of this state of life in terms of its virtues—the qualities of our Buddha nature are the qualities that make human beings truly great.

In his letter "The Three Kinds of Treasure," Nichiren wrote: "More valuable than treasures in a storehouse are the treasures of the body, and the treasures of the heart are the most valuable of all. From the time you read this letter on, strive to accumulate the treasures of the heart!"

Treasures of the storehouse are material possessions and financial wealth. Treasures of the body are health, good appearance, knowledge, status, etc. While these are important and neglecting them would cause us unnecessary suffering, they are all subject to the law of impermanence, and hence they are ultimately relative. They change with time and cannot be the foundation of lasting happiness.

Treasures of the heart means treasures of the inner realm, qualities and attributes arising from our Buddha nature. The real treasures of life are those qualities that enhance our actions in daily life, giving us the wisdom, courage and confidence to win over any circumstance. The foundation of human happiness begins in the inner realm. Happiness constructed here is not dependent, transient or circumstantial—it is resilient and, as Hamlet put it, resistant to the "slings and arrows of outrageous fortune."

Nichiren referred to this inner realm as the "treasure tower" (another name for Buddhahood). He wrote: "No treasure tower exists other than the figures of the men and women who embrace the Lotus Sutra. It follows, therefore, that whether eminent or humble, high or low, those who chant Nam-myoho-renge-kyo are themselves the treasure tower…. The place where you chant [Nam-myoho-renge-kyo] will become the dwelling place of the treasure tower."

The treasures of the heart (the qualities of absolute happiness, the attributes of the Buddha) are stored in the treasure tower of human life. We human beings are the treasure towers. By chanting Nam-myoho-renge-kyo we can recognize that we are endowed with everything we need to be absolutely happy; we can open the treasure tower of our lives; and we can revitalize ourselves by manifesting those treasures in our daily lives.

How do you begin? You start by chanting Nam-myoho-renge-kyo. Over and over again. You chant in the morning. You chant in the evening. You chant when you are blue. You chant when you are happy. You chant prodigious amounts (an hour or more) when you are facing a challenge or a crisis. And then changes begin to occur. The more one chants, the more his or her dominant life tendency becomes that of Buddhahood.

Buddhahood is not a remote destination, some inaccessible mountain peak that can only be scaled after many decades, perhaps even many lifetimes, of arduous effort. On the contrary, Nichiren explained it as the goal of one's daily practice.

Think of an iron chip becoming magnetized by constantly rubbing up against a magnet: the iron chip acquires north and south poles and the power to attract other iron filings through that exchange. The more we chant sincerely, the more our lives begin to take on the "magnetism" of enlightenment. Through chanting Nam-myoho-renge kyo (rubbing against the magnet), we gain wisdom and life force (become magnetized) and attract good fortune and protection by being in harmony with our environment.

For example, in the state of Anger, the condition itself is transformed, so that the anger expresses itself in a way that produces value—perhaps, in the form of indignation against injustice. Tranquility, in a moment of crisis, takes on the virtue of patience.

Developing the Inner Self

Contemporary researchers in the field of psychology tell us that to be happy one must: (1) have self-esteem, (2) feel in control of one's life, (3) have an optimistic outlook, and (4) be committed to a noble purpose. In addition to these inner qualities researchers also concur that having (5) meaningful work and play and (6) maintaining lasting, loving relationships are also important components of living happily. (More on these last two in the next chapter.)

The best predictor of general life satisfaction, according to a nationwide study conducted by the University of Michigan, is not satisfaction with family life, friendships

or income but satisfaction with self. As Daisaku Ikeda
has written:

> True happiness is not the absence of suffering: You
> cannot have day after day of clear skies. True hap-
> piness lies in building a self that stands dignified
> and indomitable. Happiness doesn't mean having a
> life free from all difficulties but that whatever
> difficulties arise, without being shaken in the least,
> you can summon up the unflinching courage and
> conviction to fight and overcome them.

Ultimately happiness is determined by the degree to
which we establish a solid self. This self is actually the
true self of one's life, the eternally existing life of Buddha
that exists in harmony with the law of the universe. As
we discover the great treasures or virtues of life through
Buddhist practice, we can foster a dramatic revision of
self-image, an awakening to our inherent greatness.

In that sense, attaining Buddhahood is a process of
discovering what currently lies dormant within our own
hearts, of discovering our true universal self. At the same
time, this is not a state of life restricted only to the inner
realm. The transformation of self-image we foster in the
depths of our lives becomes manifest in our behavior as

well as in our environment. In our bodies and minds, our relationships and our surroundings, chanting Nam-myoho-renge-kyo moves our universe with enormous power toward happiness.

By carrying out Buddhist practice, we say that one can bring forth the highest state of life, absolute happiness or Buddhahood. Because this happiness is constructed within, it cannot be destroyed by ever-changing circumstances without. It liberates us from dependency on external events and is a form of ultimate control or self-mastery, an important aspect of happiness.

"Hell is to drift, heaven is to steer," wrote George Bernard Shaw. Those who engage in the study and practice of Buddhism gain ever-increasing control over their inner state and, consequently, control of their exterior circumstances. They literally take charge of their own universe, becoming masters of their fate by mastering their own minds.

Even outside the world of Buddhist philosophy, the notion of self-mastery or control is recognized as an important ingredient in happiness. And, according to the Michigan study, the fifteen percent of the population who felt in control of their lives had "extraordinary positive feelings of happiness." Among these people, three in five—double the national average—reported being "very happy." Those who had a strong "internal locus of control" typically achieved more in school, coped better with stress, and lived more happily.

To see how this works in Buddhism, let's examine a real-life experience, that of a young woman who began her Buddhist practice in particularly miserable circumstances. She had a lifelong pattern of failed relationships and jobs. She was deeply discouraged about her future and depressed most of the time. She was in a state of Hell without hope.

She tentatively began to chant Nam-myoho-renge-kyo, focusing on a lasting relationship and a meaningful career. Although improvement was made on both fronts, failure continued to plague her. But self-knowledge began to develop. She gradually recognized the root of her problem: self-hatred. Her inner critic constantly pestered her with thoughts of self-doubt and worthlessness.

After chanting for a period following a particularly heart-rending breakup, she kept wondering: "Why doesn't anyone love me? What's wrong with me?" As she continued her practice, she realized that no one could love her because she didn't love herself. From that point forward she focused her practice on seeing her true self, her great qualities, her Buddha nature. She came to accept her weaknesses as natural and to witness and acknowledge her unique and wonderful assets. The more she loved and appreciated herself, the more her environment began to reflect that inner change.

Her professional relationships developed for the better, and she became increasingly trusted and valued at work. This led to new opportunities and financial rewards. She nurtured an old relationship back to health and is now happily married with two children. It all began with taking control of and developing her inner self, the foundation of inner happiness.

Optimism: The Dawn of Hope

Tapping our absolute happiness also means living optimistically. Optimists are healthier and more successful. "No empowerment is so effective as self-empowerment," wrote Harvard University historian and economist David S. Landes in his 1999 book, *The Wealth and Poverty of Nations: Why Some Are So Rich and Some So Poor.* "In this world, the optimists have it, not because they are always right, but because they are always positive. Even when wrong, they are positive, and that is the way to achievement."

Buddhism teaches us to regard everything in a positive light, as an opportunity for growth, as the raw material for developing absolute happiness. Chanting Nam-myoho-renge-kyo is the wellspring of this optimism and growth, what Buddhism calls "value creation." This wellspring enables practitioners to turn everything in their lives, joys and sufferings alike, into causes for absolute happiness. As a result, individuals develop confidence in their power to transform even intense suffering into the raw material of happiness. With this power, everything is a benefit, an opportunity.

Let's turn to another real-life example. One fifty-eight-year-old engineering executive and Buddhist practitioner, who had devoted his entire career to a large company, found his happiness and self-confidence seriously tested when he lost his job as a result of downsizing.

At his age, his job prospects were poor. Although he made extraordinary efforts to look for work, weeks turned into months with no job on the horizon. Family savings were exhausted, bills were unpaid.

But the real challenge was that he began to lose hope. This loss of hope drained him of the determination and energy necessary to investigate and prepare for a new career. He was confronted with the prospect of losing everything for which he had worked. He came face to face with the fickle nature of a happiness based on success, status and material wealth.

He sought spiritual counseling from other experienced Buddhists and learned to see his situation as an opportunity to develop a more solid foundation for his inner life, to pursue the treasures of the heart rather than those of the storehouse. He realized that he had been neglecting his family and other important relationships as well as his health and personal growth. He had been, in effect, trading gold for dross.

He focused his chanting, using this crisis as an opportunity to set a new course in life with his priorities straight. He began to see his problem as an important opportunity. With this shift of perspective, renewed optimism and determination began to flow from deep within his life. This filled him with fresh energy and a willingness to seek opportunities in directions he had previously not considered.

Almost immediately, an entry-level opportunity opened in a completely new field. He investigated and found it surprisingly exciting. There were possibilities for unlimited advancement. He eventually developed a highly successful new career that became far more fulfilling than the work he had done before. More important, his newfound success did not distract him from his commitment to self-development, family and friends. He kept his life in balance and found a happiness he never realized was possible.

As Daisaku Ikeda has written: "True joy emerges ceaselessly from within your life while you squarely battle to overcome each storm of hardships. This kind of true joy gushes forth endlessly. You cannot enjoy a true and profound joy if you seek only to indulge yourself in comfortable situations where you don't have to experience severe hardships."

Living With Purpose and Meaning Makes Us Strong

We are strong, and we are weak; none of us are totally one or the other. Simply put, we are strong when we have something important to do. And we are weak when we have nothing meaningful to do. The weakness we observe in those whose lives are ruled by obsessions and addictions is the symptom of a deeply rooted purposelessness that permeates our society. "To be filled each day with a rewarding sense of exhilaration and purpose," Ikeda wrote, "a sense of tasks accomplished and deep fulfillment — people who feel this way are happy."

Real happiness is linked to pledging oneself to a great purpose. One who lives this way is strong, strong enough to be happy under any circumstances. One who lives this way experiences a sense of fulfillment in the depths of life unaffected by the surrounding constant change. "Of course," Ikeda continues, "the mission or objective that you have taken on yourself must be in accord with the happiness of oneself and others. That is what makes absolute happiness possible."

The Buddhism of Nichiren teaches the necessity of a "you and me" outlook. Thus, Buddhists practice to become happy themselves and, at the same time, to help others become happy and bring peace to society, recognizing that it is ultimately impossible to build personal happiness on the sufferings (or unhappiness) of others. Furthermore, efforts for the happiness of others become an important source of one's own happiness. Therefore it is the greatest and noblest mission to make efforts for the sake of others. In doing so, the selfish ego recedes and the true self, or Buddhahood, comes to the forefront.

There are, of course, many ways to act compassionately toward others. The discipline of Buddhism includes both practice for oneself and practice for others, with the idea that giving others the means to continually enhance their own capacity to overcome misery and become absolutely happy is the ultimate compassionate act.

We chant for the happiness of others. We teach others how to chant. And we study Buddhism together, those more experienced sharing their knowledge and insights — and, in turn, having their practice refreshed by the realizations of newcomers. We continually work to expand our ability to create harmony with others in all our environment — among family, friends, coworkers, neighbors and so on.

Fulfillment arises from recognizing this mission of helping others realize their potential and from exerting oneself to make it a reality. Living without compassion is a shallow existence. The Bodhisattva way, the path of helping others, is the certain path to absolute happiness. To quote George Bernard Shaw again, from *Man and Superman*:

> This is the true joy in life, the being used for a purpose recognized by yourself as a mighty one; the being thoroughly worn out before you are thrown on the scrap heap; the being a force of nature instead of a feverish selfish clod of ailments and grievances complaining that the world will not devote itself to make you happy.

In this sense, real happiness is not about simply having lofty ideals, but about taking action to fulfill one's purpose or mission in life on behalf of others. Victor Hugo's last written words were, "To love is to act." Similarly we might say, "To be happy is to act."

As Nichiren stated: "The purpose of the appearance in this world of Shakyamuni Buddha, the lord of teachings, lies in his behavior as a human being. The wise may be called human, but the thoughtless are no more than animals." Shakyamuni's unceasing actions to bring other human beings to enlightenment, to share his Buddhahood in the most *thoughtful* way possible, according to the capacity of his audiences — "his behavior as a human being" — was as important as anything he actually said.

Chanting Nam-myoho-renge-kyo for yourself and for others is the "secret" for becoming absolutely happy in this world. As Nichiren wrote, "There is no true happiness for human beings other than chanting Nam-myoho-renge-kyo." Chanting Nam-myoho-renge-kyo awakens the compassionate impulse that is dormant within, bringing forth the higher life-condition toward which we need to sincerely strive. Our happiness depends on our promoting the happiness of others.

Human Transformation

Based on the teaching of the Ten Worlds, Buddhism explains that the way to achieve absolute happiness in this lifetime—in this world, and in our present circumstances —is by taking charge of our inner state of life. Unaware of the Ten Worlds within (especially our inherent Buddha nature), we waste enormous amounts of energy pursuing relative happiness.

What keeps people in the lower six worlds are delusions arising from what Buddhism terms the "three poisons"—*greed*, *anger* and *foolishness*. Allowing the three poisons free reign—for example, believing that acquisition will lead one to happiness—will actually trap us in the lower states, where continued suffering and unhappiness are the only possible results.

If delusions are the cause of unhappiness and believing in a correct philosophy will lead one to absolute happiness, then reforming incorrect beliefs becomes the practical method for pursuing happiness. Thus Nichiren concluded that if we wish to become happy we should "quickly reform the tenets we hold in our hearts" and embrace the wisdom of Buddhism.

Buddhist practice is designed to help us reform the deluded tenets in our hearts. This process of inner reformation, human revolution, unlike revolutions of the past, involves no ideologies, moral systems, codes of behavior or violence. We simply chant Nam-myoho-renge-kyo with an expectation of benefit, a hope that our life goals might be achieved.

Whether we feel happy or unhappy ultimately depends on us. Without changing our state of life, we cannot find true happiness. But when we do change our inner state, our whole world is transformed. The means for accomplishing this transformation is chanting Nam-myoho-renge-kyo, the cornerstone of the Buddhist practice. We chant Nam-myoho-renge-kyo to achieve our human revolution, to reform the beliefs we harbor, and to summon the inner strength to transcend our personal difficulties and help others.

FIVE

RELATIONSHIPS
THAT
WORK

The greater my love of mankind in general,
the less I love people in particular,
that is to say, separately, as individuals.
—Fyodor Dostoevsky

I define love thus: the will to extend one's
self for the purpose of nurturing one's own
or another's spiritual growth.
—M. Scott Peck

To LOVE PEOPLE or to cherish humanity in the abstract is relatively easy. To feel compassion toward real individuals, to love a single human being, is considerably more difficult. Most of us have heard stories of individuals who support worthy social causes, perhaps funding philanthropic organizations or even social activist groups, but whose private lives are characterized by insensitivity, even cruelty to those close to them. By contrast, compassion for humanity in Buddhist teachings is not mere idealism — it is something we strive for every day.

We have said that the Buddha nature dwells within each individual and that one's happiness is based on building a solid inner self. Though Buddhism is a powerful tool for building inner strength, it is not a solitary activity. Rather, the Buddhist teaching shows that compassionate interaction with others is the most satisfying way to live in society and is, in fact, a virtual prerequisite for enlightenment.

A person of wisdom tries to invigorate and bring out the best in others. The humanism of the Lotus Sutra, the core teaching for this modern age, comes down to treasuring the individual. A person in the state of Buddhahood respects others' individuality, and desires that they manifest their unique qualities as well. The Buddhist objective of universal enlightenment thus begins with treasuring the self, then the individuals around us, finally extending outward to encompass all people.

How to cultivate this attitude and develop fulfilling relationships is the subject of this chapter.

One thing is certain, everybody has relationships. Even those living a monastic life interact with other monks. Relationships of various kinds are an inevitable part of human life, all the more so for people living amid the daily realities of family, partnerships and work. But beyond this, the desire for companionship is very deeply rooted. In their pursuit of personal happiness, human beings are driven in the pursuit of lasting and fulfilling relationships, especially intimate ones.

Having satisfying, enduring relationships contributes greatly to our happiness. All too often, unfortunately, relationships—whether with family, friends or coworkers—

can be a source of suffering and pain more than of joy and fulfillment. Or relationships that were once fulfilling don't last. Given that so many sincere and well-intentioned people exert so much effort and energy in seeking and nurturing relationships, why is it that so many of them fail?

They fail because we lack the wisdom to make them work. Frequently, we enter into them for reasons not conducive to their survival.

It's All Up to You

Whether you experience a relationship in a positive or negative way is determined by you — by your own beliefs and attitudes. This idea may at first seem hard to accept. Nonetheless, developing successful relationships begins with accepting full responsibility for your life and your role in those relationships.

"It's hard to soar like an eagle," reads a familiar bumper sticker, "when you're surrounded by turkeys." Buddhism teaches that one's environment reflects his or her inner state of life. Buddhism suggests that if you are surrounded by turkeys, it's very likely that instead of the eagle you may think yourself to be, you are, in fact, a turkey yourself. And, by extension, your environment is a turkey farm. The problem is not, however, that your fellow turkeys are preventing you from soaring. Rather, it is that you must transform yourself into the eagle you desire to be.

As each of us is, at the most essential level, a Buddha, there is nothing wrong with us. We are not impure or flawed. It is our unenlightened mind that is flawed. This is not the same as saying that the victim is at fault. Certainly there are people behaving badly, causing others, perhaps you, to suffer. We are not, however, responsible for the behavior of others, only for ourselves. When you understand this, you will realize there is something ultimately liberating in this idea: Since we control the choices in our own lives, we have the power to do something about our unsatisfactory relationships.

Nichiren taught that sufferings arise from "looking outside of oneself" for the cause or the solution to problems. The fact that it is you who are suffering means it is your problem to solve, not someone else's. If you're looking for others to change, you may wait a very long time. Still, people make extraordinary efforts to modify the behavior of others in an effort to make relationships work. But ultimately this is as futile as cleaning the mirror in an attempt to clean your face. The mirror will just keep reflecting back the same image.

Through Buddhist practice, we start to see ourselves more accurately perhaps for the first time in our lives, with all our weaknesses and strengths. Day after day, we come to an ever-deepening realization (although sudden, remarkable flashes of self-realization are quite common) that the relationships we have formed are a reflection of our own state of life. Then we can embark on the steady, long-term process of developing our wisdom and capacity as human beings.

The key to transforming relationships lies in the process of transforming ourselves. Since the only person whose behavior you control is yourself, use that power to the utmost. Work from the inside out.

Buddhism teaches that false attitudes or beliefs about the self and others, which lead to misery and suffering, can be traced to the "three poisons": greed, anger and foolishness. In particular, anger, the poison compounded of equal measures of arrogance and self-centeredness, destroys relationships. The poison of anger leads inevitably to strife and conflict among people, whether individuals, groups or nations. War has its roots in the poison of anger.

Buddhism calls the poisoned self, the arrogant, self-regarding egomaniac within us all, the lesser self. The ultimate purpose of Buddhist practice is to manifest a

greater or true self. Understanding the purpose of relationships and purifying ourselves of the three poisons go
hand in hand.

The Perfect Relationship:
Two People Standing Alone Together

A Buddhist teacher once explained that there are three
stages in the character development of human beings:
dependent, independent and contributive. Unfortunately, most people are completely unaware of the third,
the contributive (or interdependent), state of life. For
them, there are only two options, independence or
dependence.

Independence, the stand-alone self, can be a happy
state because we are in control, a necessary condition
of happiness. The strong, confident self, however, can
easily become arrogant and isolated. But arrogance and
companionship don't mix well. It is all too likely that an
arrogant person will be unable to sustain fulfilling relationships. Instead, those relationships will most often
end in conflict and strife.

The alternative for most is dependent (or codepen-
dent) relationships. People give respect and love, but not
freely; strings are attached. This is the let's-make-a-deal

approach to relationships, "I'll love you as long as you give me what I need."

Life in this sort of relationship can only be an emotional roller coaster, climbing to exhilarating highs and plunging into desperate lows. This is because your happiness is dependent upon another's behavior — upon his or her validation of your worthiness of being loved.

Happiness in any situation cannot be achieved without a sense of control. Depending upon another to validate that we are worthy of love gives that person control over our emotions and our self-esteem. We have given up our power.

Janet's Experience: My Husband's Drinking Problem

Janet had been struggling in her marriage for many years. Her husband's drinking had caused her immense suffering, not only physically and emotionally but spiritually as well. She tried reasoning with him. She tried improving herself, to be a better wife. She felt unable to effect change even though she made effort. This led her to great self-doubt and a critical view of life. She gave up hope that her husband would stop drinking or that she would have a happy marriage.

Janet considered leaving him, but the idea of being alone frightened her. At some level, her husband knew she would never leave because she was dependent, financially and emotionally, on him. So she stayed, year after year after year.

Since, after all, his drinking was the problem, it never dawned on her that she needed to change anything about herself. After much sincere searching for a solution, she became hopelessly resigned to her situation, too weak to muster the determination to do anything about her unhappiness. Not surprisingly, things got worse.

Finally, a friend introduced Janet to Nichiren Buddhism. She began her practice in earnest, chanting Nam-myoho-renge-kyo each day. In the ensuing weeks, in addition to several conspicuous benefits, she came to a big realization: she was trying to change the wrong person. She had been convinced that all her efforts needed to be focused on getting her husband to alter his behavior, and until he did, she would continue on in misery.

As she began to learn more about Buddhist philosophy and to tap into her Buddha wisdom, it occurred to her that she needed to become happy herself regardless of whether her husband ever stopped drinking. She awakened to the fact that she'd been disrespecting herself by allowing herself to be unhappy.

By developing a stronger inner self through her Buddhist practice, Janet's behavior toward her husband (which had been fueled by anger and frustration) changed, and genuine concern for his happiness came forth from her heart. As she chanted for the happiness of both of them, strength and determination were kindled and fueled within her. She came to understand that as partners they were facilitating each other to be weak and dependent. Finally, her resolve solidified and she spoke to her husband.

This time she approached him differently, not out of fear or anger and without the implied message that he had to change on her behalf. She said: "I am sorry that drinking is a problem for you, but I will no longer involve myself in it. My responsibility is to my own happiness, and I hope my own peace of mind will help you, too." With this new, genuine approach came a surprising response from her husband — he took her seriously. Finally, he could hear her. That night he stopped drinking.

Even better, beyond his return to sobriety there quickly came a deeper change in their relationship. They released their dependent hold upon each other and replaced it with the beginnings of an interdependent, contributive life together. They started experiencing a degree of happiness they had both felt was forever beyond their reach. Her inner breakthrough — her new-found strength, wisdom and determination uncovered through Buddhist practice — was the key to initiating a life-altering external breakthrough.

So is it our partners' fault if we are unhappy? In a superficial sense, perhaps. But essentially this is dictated by us, by the extent to which we persist in giving our partner the final say over our happiness — whether our partner wants it or not — and by the extent to which we believe we cannot be happy without the help or change in behavior of another.

Now, you may ask, what if Janet's husband hadn't stopped drinking? She said she would have felt sorry on his behalf, but she was prepared to be happy whether he stopped or not, even if it meant leaving. She was no longer willing to depend on him and his behavior for her happiness. And she realized how unhappy he was with their situation as well. This woman had been giving away her power. Her husband's behavior had become the determining factor in their relationship. Her strong resolve to become absolutely happy in the face of everything liberated both of them from their mutual dependency.

In any relationship, we must keep our power, developing a strong self-identity and the ability to be happy on the inside. Standing alone upon the firm foundation of our own happiness, we can then seek out and nurture contributive, sharing relationships, relationships in which we give our love freely without attachments and expectations. We are not needy of the other. Nor are we addicted to the other. A relationship between two such people brings a deep and abiding love.

Before going out to look for a contributive partner, we must first strive to develop that ability within ourselves. Only then will it be possible to draw forth and nurture the same quality in others. "Happiness is not something that someone else, like a boyfriend or girlfriend, can give to us," Daisaku Ikeda wrote in his book *The Way of Youth*. "We have to achieve it for ourselves. And the only way to do so is by developing our character and capacity as human beings, by fully realizing our own potential. If we sacrifice our growth and talent for love, we absolutely will not find happiness."

Finding the Right Relationship: Tend to the Garden

At this point you might say: "My problem is not how to fix a broken relationship; my problem is that I don't *have* a relationship. If I had one, then I could work on it." This is a common lament. But actually we all have lots of relationships, and we don't really know how they may develop. There are many stories of people finding that a close friendship unexpectedly turns to romance or a working relationship develops into something deeper. You can never be sure where, how or when the "relationship of your life" may blossom.

Finding success in relationships is not, as pop culture would have it, like clothes shopping: checking out all the outfits (possible partners) until we find just the right one, returning those that don't fit or discarding them when they go out of style. Rather, the process is more like moving into a new house and finding a long-untended garden in the back. Carefully we nurture the many unfamiliar plants that we find there, patiently waiting to see what fruits and blossoms come forth in their own time. Not being sure how or when they will blossom, we nurture them all, enjoying the process of discovery as each blossoms in its own beautiful way. The goal is to be a master gardener of relationships.

As with gardening, there can be much enjoyment and satisfaction in this process. Expecting relationships to bear fruit immediately is unrealistic and actually counterproductive to establishing a long-term bond. Relationships are like seedlings—nurture them all and take pleasure as they grow, blossom and bear fruit. Too often we discard seedling relationships before ever seeing their possibilities. That's not to say we can't continually add to the garden. There will always be many more wonderful relationships, an endless supply, for us to develop. But rather than continually looking for the "right" relationship, it's more important to cultivate the ones you already have. Somewhere in the garden of your life, incredible things wait to bloom.

While we enter romantic relationships because we are in love with the other person, it is important to view all of our relationships as fertile ground for the growth, development, maturation and strengthening of our own character. The self-actualization we undergo in a good relationship makes us happy, not the relationship itself. This kind of growth and emotional development is termed *human revolution*, whereby the practice of Buddhism fosters an inner transformation. The Chinese characters for this concept depict transformation occurring in the space between people. Transformation is the result of interacting with others with the intention of fostering mutual growth. Our growth is an interdependent process.

In the story told above, it was the woman's inner transformation that led to a positive result. She might have opted simply to leave her husband, but in doing so she would have missed the opportunity for personal growth, which led to her greater happiness and sense of fulfillment. By sidestepping that growth, she would have brought the very same delusions and weaknesses to future relationships, reliving her suffering over and over again.

The Looking-Outside-of-Oneself Delusion

Hell in relationships comes from trying to change the behavior of anyone other than yourself. When we exercise self-control, beginning with becoming happy within ourselves, we have the ability to move the hearts of others. It is only when we stop trying to control others that we gain the power to actually influence them. For example, have you ever found yourself saying "You're making me angry—stop doing that" to people whose behavior disturbs or frustrates you? The implication of that statement, "you're making me angry," is that somehow you don't have control of your anger. They do. And since you have ceded them the control and power, it is their behavior that must change if your anger is to be eliminated. But, of course, you don't control their behavior, so the more you try to do so, the angrier you get.

Not that all anger is bad. There are, of course, real situations of injustice in which anger is appropriate. Even in such cases, however, self-control is the key to influencing change. Buddhism teaches us that in response to any situation, depending on the choices we make, we find ourselves in one of the Ten Worlds: Hell, Hunger, Animality, Anger, Tranquility, Rapture, Learning, Realization, Bodhisattva or Buddhahood. Recognizing that we are choosing and taking responsibility for those choices empowers us to choose our life state. It gives us our control back.

Timothy's Experience: I'm Right But Losing

The dilemma of a young man practicing Buddhism in Seattle provides a case in point. Although Timothy was a bright, personable and successful individual, his relationship with his wife caused him much suffering. His wife was convinced, based on circumstantial evidence, that he was being unfaithful to her. He knew he was innocent of such behavior. Yet she remained convinced, and his adamant denials only convinced her further.

Though intelligent and perceptive, he could not understand the root cause of his problems at home. As a result, the marriage and family that meant everything to him were disintegrating. He was perpetually angry.

Based on advice from friends and counselors, he expressed his anger. He didn't keep it in. But things got worse. Then he tried, again following advice from others, to keep his anger in check and not express it. That didn't help either. He seemed destined to lose the most important people in his life due to "irreconcilable differences." Timothy was facing the prospect of divorce and separation from his children.

The key point for him was that he was "right." The specific situation at the root of the arguments was a misperception of events on his wife's part. She was quite simply "wrong." Yet, he was suffering (as was she). He seemed to have lost any ability to change his life (or, more specifically, his wife). As in our earlier story, he was trying to change the wrong person, although on the surface a change in his wife would have been the easiest solution. His frustration arose from the fact that he was powerless (as are we all) to compel change in another person. What to do?

Timothy had believed deeply that his wife was making him angry. In that sense, he had been blinded by his "rightness." Thinking that being right was a justification for his anger, he continued to confront his wife. Fortunately, he continued to seek a deeper understanding through Buddhist practice, study and consultation. He came to realize he was "looking outside of himself."

As he continued to chant Nam-myoho-renge-kyo, Timothy eventually realized that he had to search for a solution within himself, his own behavior, the only area actually within his control. As he did so, he saw that he indeed bore responsibility for the deterioration of the situation. While his wife may have been in the wrong, at the same time he was compounding the error by adding the poison of his own anger. Thus, relatively simple misunderstandings quickly degenerated into violent storms, fueled mostly by his own contributions. In other words, he was both right and wrong. He realized that his wife's accusations arose from an underlying lack of confidence and self-esteem that were exacerbated by his angry outbursts.

Recognizing his complicity in the conflict, Timothy focused his Buddhist practice on his own responsibility rather than expecting his wife to change first. By this time, his problems had spread to the workplace and to his friendships. He found himself in the right most of the time in terms of specific events but angry and increasingly isolated as well. It wasn't a matter of saying he was wrong when he knew he was right, which in any case would have gone against his nature.

Instead, it was a matter of learning to be right wisely.

As he developed greater wisdom and self-control, chanting to respond compassionately to the mistakes of others, he found himself in charge of his own emotional state. He began to recognize the foolishness of believing that anyone could make him angry if he chose not to be. As a result, the relationship that was nearly destroyed began, once again, to flourish and eventually blossomed into a beautiful and harmonious partnership. While his wife's suspicions did not stop immediately, they no longer had the power to upset his emotional state. In the absence of his anger, which had been fueling them, they diminished to the point of insignificance and eventually disappeared altogether.

Comparing ourselves with others is another variation of the looking-outside delusion. There's an old adage that says "you can't tell a book by its cover." You can't tell much about a person's life — if it's getting better or worse, if they're happy or unhappy — by looking at externals. The only meaningful comparison one can make is the comparison between our life today and yesterday, last month or last year. Wall Street analysts, for example, don't generally compare IBM to General Motors or Amazon.com to AT&T. They compare each company's quarterly earnings to the quarter before, and to the same period a year before, assessing how the company is growing relative to past performance. Similarly, if things are better in your life than they were, then you have the best kind of life, an improving, growing life. As we have said earlier in this book, you can't tell much about your own life by looking at the lives of others. That's why growth is so important. Life changes constantly. It is the nature of the cosmos to change. Therefore, even if we could create circumstances of complete happiness, we can only look forward to them changing. The ability to grow with those changes is real happiness.

Ultimately, we create true happiness by developing our lives to the fullest. Trying to be somebody else or what you think somebody else wants you to be is a sure way to suffer. Be who you are and be it well. Be where you are and be there well. If you are continually growing and advancing, you have the greatest life in the world because you know tomorrow will always be better than today.

The Downside of Expectations

Expectations are important. Research indicates that children develop only as far as the expectations of the adults around them. But expectations can also destroy perfectly good relationships. We have expectations of other people. We expect them to be good husbands, good wives, good children, good friends, good bosses and so on. These expectations are often unrealistically high, sometimes higher than our expectations of ourselves.

Let's imagine a relationship where the initial passions have faded. The honeymoon is over. Now the bride and groom are awakening to the fact that their respective partner is not perfect. Let's say he or she is only about eighty percent OK. Partners have flaws and imperfections, as we all do, they reason. Because they care about each other and about their happiness together, they want and expect each other to do better, to improve themselves. Each expects the other to bridge the gap and become the ideal partner.

Motivated by their love, they begin to tell each other, in the most affectionate and caring way possible, about the twenty percent that is missing. Each believes that the love that exists between them will motivate the other to strive harder to fill the gap. Because they are motivated by love, with only the best intentions, they are surprised to find that after an initial period of positive response things get progressively worse. Why? Where did the love go?

Does this scenario sound familiar? Do you know a couple that began deeply in love but ended not so many years later in acrimonious divorce? How does this happen to people? While every situation is unique, there is at least one common but subtle delusion at work here, a delusion that is a challenge to all of us in our relationships with significant others, children, family, friends. The problem is that although we are motivated by the best intentions, the other person often hears from us a steady stream of criticism and disappointment. This is not encouraging, and in spite of the love in our hearts, the other person becomes unresponsive, even rebellious. The problem here is that although the heart is in the right place, we lack wisdom. Motivated by love but lacking wisdom, we get a response to our efforts that is the opposite of what we expected. Once this downward trend begins, unfortunately, it is often difficult to reverse.

People do not respond well to constant criticism and negativity. Does that mean we simply have to settle for something less? No, it means, once again, that we're trying to change the wrong person. If we want people to do more, we need to praise and appreciate what they are already doing for us. In other words, it's the eighty percent that is happening that should be the focus of our attention, not the twenty percent that's missing! People love praise and appreciation and will try very hard to get them. Making these two the basis of all your relationships can have a powerful and encouraging influence. For the gardener of relationships, they are like sunlight and water. People will strive and thrive when they are praised and appreciated.

Criticism and disappointment create a dark environment, a garden where relationships cannot thrive. It is a major delusion to think that others will be motivated by criticism. Nichiren wrote: "When praised, one does not consider his personal risk, and when criticized, he can recklessly cause his own ruin. Such is the way of common mortals."

Work and Career

Work and the relationships we form there are an important arena in the struggle for enlightenment. In a sense, the affairs of life and work are the testing ground of one's practice. What career one chooses has little to do with one's happiness. It's not what we do for a living but how we do it and whether we feel useful and find meaning in our work that make the difference. Therefore, while we should chant abundantly to take a career path that is true to what's in our hearts, tormenting oneself about the selection of a career is, to some degree, irrelevant to establishing a happy life.

This is not to say that there aren't a lot of unhappy people in the workplace. There are. But it's not the work that's to blame; it is the people who bring with them attitudes and beliefs about work that are not conducive to a happy, fulfilling experience.

Tsunesaburo Makiguchi, the first president of the Soka Gakkai (the lay organization of Nichiren Buddhists in Japan; see Chapter 8 for information on the American organization, the SGI-USA), taught that there are three kinds of value: beauty, gain and good. The perfect job would have all three. In the working world, the value of beauty means finding a job you like; the value of gain or benefit is a job that earns you a salary to support your daily life; the value of good means a job that helps others and contributes to society. The ideal job would be one that you like, that offers financial security, where you can contribute to society. Sounds great. But this is seldom the reality. Not many can find the perfect job from the start. Some may have a job they like, but it isn't putting food on the table; or their job may pay well, but they hate it. That's the way things go sometimes. Also, some discover that they're just not cut out for the career they dreamed of and aspired to.

The most important thing in finding satisfaction at work is becoming indispensable wherever you are. The

best way to find the best job is to become the best employee. Good circumstances don't make good people;
good people make for a good workplace atmosphere. By
learning to be an exemplary individual at work, opportunities will present themselves, opening a path leading
to your next phase of life, during which you should also
continue doing your very best. Such continuous efforts
are guaranteed to land you jobs that you like, that support your life and that allow you to contribute to society.
Then, when you look back later, you will see how all your
past efforts have become precious assets in your ideal
field. You will realize that your effort and hardships have
not been wasted.

In real estate it's said that the three most important
things are location, location, location. In finding happiness at work the three most important things are attitude, attitude, attitude. To the first important principle
about succeeding at work, becoming indispensable, we'd
like to add a second: creating harmony on the job.

When working at a company, which is like a society
or community all its own, it is important to create harmonious relations with all of your colleagues, including
your superiors and those working under you, using wisdom and discretion along the way. If you incur your
coworkers' dislike by being selfish or egoistic, you will

be a loser in work and society. Wisdom, which includes tact, is vital to being successful at one's work.

Brandon's Experience: "Bad Money Karma"

Several years ago, Brandon, a young man of thirty, sought advice from a fellow Buddhist in changing what he called his "bad money karma." He was desperate. He had recently quit his job and was on the verge of losing his home, and his wife was considering leaving with the children due to his financial irresponsibility. He was very clear about needing a job—one that would pay him lots of money—right away. He wanted to know how to chant to accomplish that goal.

Brandon was told that chanting Nam-myoho-renge-kyo is not a magic formula like abracadabra (although it sometimes seems that way). That would be fairy-tale Buddhism. He was surprised and a bit discouraged at this news. He was asked about his work experience and how he had gotten himself into such a crisis. He admitted that he couldn't seem to keep a job for long. He had had eight jobs in less than ten years. "Why do I have such bad job karma?" he wondered. "The jobs I get always look good at first but never work out for some reason. How can I chant to get a better, longer-lasting job?"

Each time he had been fired or quit a position it was because of a boss. He just wasn't getting along with them. Did Brandon see a pattern in these events? "Oh, yes," he said, "What I really want to know is why I have such bad boss karma. Every boss I've ever had has been authoritarian and impossible to work with. How can I chant to get a better boss?"

Brandon was a highly educated computer programmer with excellent credentials. His Buddhist confidant told him about the role of the lesser self in destroying harmony in relationships, explaining that one of the most important qualities of a good employee is the ability to work with others and to take direction from supervisors (who directly or indirectly control paychecks). His advisor pointed out that the pattern of failed jobs, bad bosses and financial instability were all symptoms of a person who cannot rise above differences in order to work with others. Although it was harsh advice, he could recognize his own arrogant, angry nature, and he admitted that this had been a problem since childhood.

He then said: "I've been thinking of starting my own business. Then I won't have to work for anyone. How can I chant to do that?" He was cautioned that owning one's own business requires even more people skills. Whether at his own business or working for someone else, he needed to transcend his self-centeredness and learn to respect others; to overcome his arrogance. If he did that, he could transform his job situation and also resolve his domestic problems since they had the same root.

His Buddhist friend also cautioned him that he would surely face another job situation where he would feel that it wasn't working out and would want to quit or confront management (his familiar behavior). When that happened, he was told, don't act. Wait and chant.

Sure enough, about three months later Brandon was ready to quit yet another job. His mentor asked him to postpone his decision for two weeks and in the meantime exert himself in his Buddhist practice with a determination to control his arrogance by respecting and listening to his boss. Brandon was encouraged to make efforts to become indispensable. He followed the advice and, much to his surprise, instead of being fired, he received a promotion. Because of his newfound stability at work, his financial situation began to improve, he and his wife reconciled, and they eventually bought a new home. All this didn't happen "miraculously" overnight. It was the result of a subtle but powerful inner shift, brought about through Buddhist practice, which gradually manifested in Brandon's environment. This is the power of human revolution.

Relationships Help Us Develop

All our relationships have a common foundation — ourselves! The internal condition of our own lives will affect all our relationships. So what we learn in the course of any one relationship will apply to the others. Just as the three poisons — greed, anger and foolishness — will manifest in all our relationships, so, too, will all our relationships be enhanced as we purify our lives through Buddhist practice. What comes into play in one realm will also be apparent in the others.

Individuals who challenge themselves to develop happy, harmonious families will find the benefits of their efforts simultaneously apparent in improvements at work. Similarly, those who learn to transcend the lesser, egoistic self at work will garner rich rewards at home.

Buddhist practice is about developing character. And relationships are the forum, the classroom, in which we learn how.

SIX

BUDDHISM
AND
HEALTH

Health is so necessary to all the duties,
as well as pleasures of life, that the crime
of squandering it is equal to the folly.
—Samuel Johnson

Nam-myoho-renge-kyo is like the roar of a lion.
What sickness can therefore be an obstacle?
—Nichiren

SHAKYAMUNI BUDDHA, although not a doctor himself, was often called "the great medicine king." Through contemplation he came to the realization that enlightenment, or Buddhahood, is the ultimate medicine, because through its virtues we draw forth the innate wisdom and life force necessary to cure our physical and mental ills. Therefore, the chief aim of Buddhist medicine is to help individuals develop their natural self-healing powers by cultivating enlightenment through their Buddhist practice.

This view is gaining widespread recognition far beyond Buddhist practitioners. The preamble to the World Health Organization charter reads, "Health is a state of complete physical, mental, and social well-being and not merely the absence of disease or infirmity."

We are all human beings, made of flesh and blood. It is an undeniable fact that no one can avoid illness at one time or another. But the roots of sickness exist in the depths of our being. From the viewpoint of Buddhism, illness cannot destroy our happiness (unless we allow it to do so) and, since the cause for illness is inherent within, the fundamental solution to illness is also within. It is important to remember this. There is, then, no reason to be controlled by illness, no reason for it to fill us with suffering, fear or distress.

Buddhism teaches us that we possess the power not only to transform the negative into a neutral state but to go beyond that to achieve a positive state. We can overcome the suffering of sickness and in so doing even the experience of sickness enriches our lives and makes them more worthwhile, providing the material for a great drama of fulfillment that unfolds day after day.

Helen Keller wrote in her autobiography, *The Story of My Life*, that "Everything has its wonders, even darkness and silence, and I learn, whatever state I may be in, therein to be content." Just as true happiness is not simply the absence of problems but an internal life state that enables us to challenge any obstacles to happiness that come our way, health is not simply the absence of illness. Rather it is a state of being that enables us to overcome illness and the obstacles to our health. The important issue is whether we defeat sickness when it comes or whether sickness defeats us. Buddhism teaches us the source of wisdom and life force necessary for defeating illness. Because both health and illness exist as potentialities within us, we can make ourselves sick, and we can make ourselves well.

A news story from recent years illustrates this truth.

At a high school football game a few people fell ill with symptoms of food poisoning. Initial questioning seemed to indicate that contaminated soft drinks were the culprit. The snack bar was closed down, and an announcement was made asking people not to drink the sodas. Soon after the announcement, spectators all over the stadium began vomiting and passing out. Many rushed from the stands to their doctors or emergency rooms. More than a hundred people were hospitalized.

The next day, it was determined that the soft drinks had nothing to do with the sickness of the initial sufferers, they had contracted a strain of the flu. As soon as this information was disseminated, sickened spectators "miraculously" got well. Their symptoms simply disappeared and even those who were hospitalized got up from their beds and left. A pathogen was not the culprit; it was merely an idea expressed in words that had an immediate and dramatic effect in both bringing on illness and in fostering recovery.

In another example, a young man with a strong Buddhist practice and excellent medical treatment recovered from cancer not only once but a second time. When his cancer recurred a third time in the blood, however, he was told it was incurable and was given only a few months to live. Although he had reversed his cancer twice, this prognosis was too much for him, and his health began to rapidly degenerate. Friends, family, even his doctors thought he was clearly dying. Then, shockingly, it was discovered that blood samples had been mixed up. He was told that there was no trace of cancer cells in his body. He quickly recovered and regained his strength.

Such is the power of belief, of what can happen when we are strongly influenced by the diagnosis of illness and what can happen when we rally ourselves, mustering our resources to overcome it.

A similar demonstration of the power of belief is the so-called placebo effect. Medical research proved long ago that inert substances can have a positive effect on patients if they believe they are receiving effective medication. In study after study a sizeable percentage of patients who are given sugar pills in lieu of medication show signs of recovery. And, remarkably, if they have been told how the medication will make them feel, they will exhibit those very effects.

The Buddhist View of Disease

Maintaining good health and overcoming illness begin with our understanding of the true nature of self. Illness can be an opportunity to build an even more solid foundation of happiness by leading us toward significant, though often difficult, life changes. As Nichiren has written, "Illness gives rise to the resolve to attain the way."

This is not to say that we forsake modern medicine for some sort of self-directed cure. Instead, Nichiren Buddhism suggests three guidelines for curing sickness: see a good doctor, get good medicine and be an excellent patient. By being an excellent patient, Nichiren is referring to an inner state of being. He presents the practice of chanting Nam-myoho-renge-kyo as the best thing we can do to purify our state of being. Nichiren wrote: "Nam-myoho-renge-kyo is like the roar of a lion. What sickness can therefore be an obstacle?"

Chanting Nam-myoho-renge-kyo is the source of the wisdom that allows us to find the right doctor and plumb the life force that will make the medicine effective. Chanting Nam-myoho-renge-kyo is healing energy itself.

The healing process begins with strengthening the confidence with which you can say to yourself: "I can defeat my sickness. I can change the poison in my body into medicine." If our condition of being is one of defeat, sickness will defeat our will to heal. If it is one of challenge, then we have maximized the possibility of recovery.

The Scientific View:
The Oneness of Mind and Body

There is mounting scientific evidence of a strong and inseparable relationship between the workings of the mind and those of the body. The belief in the dualistic separation of mind and body that strongly influenced early medical science is gradually giving way to a deeper perspective, a view that matches very closely the Buddhist view of the oneness of mind and body.

Actually the Japanese word here translated as "oneness" is best understood as "two but not two" (see pp. 70–71), in the sense that while the mind and the body appear at some level to be two distinct phenomena, at a more profound level they are not two but one.

How does the oneness of mind and body work? Scientists have found that environmental stimuli are processed by the brain triggering complex bioelectric and biochemical reactions in the body, which in turn trigger behavior. In the case of illness, the sequence goes something like this:

As an environmental stimulus is perceived and processed by the brain (consciously and unconsciously), that process is strongly influenced by one's beliefs, ideas and expectations. This triggers a complex biological reaction (e.g., in the hypothalamus, neuro-endocrine reaction and hormone release) affecting the body's immune response determining the "capacity" to deal with disease. This results in physical symptoms, behavior and the actual experience of illness (runny nose, headache, stiff joints).

Since ideas, expectations and beliefs have a powerful effect on the workings of the body, distorted thinking (delusion) necessarily will have a powerful impact on one's health and capacity to overcome illness.

Psychologists have identified various life views that can undermine one's health, impede the body's capacity to conquer illness and lead to psychological and spiritual maladies including depression, anxiety and fear. Among them are: holding others responsible for your own pain; interpreting others' unknowable thoughts and actions in a way that is negative toward you or believing others think more strongly about you than is actually the case; and deducing fatalistic general conclusions based on specific occurrences or limited information.

Thus, in addition to medical treatment, a change of

thinking is crucial in overcoming illness. The challenge is not merely to identify distorted thinking but to change that way of thinking and accomplish a paradigm shift. It is Buddhist practice that enables us to make this shift.

The Buddhist View of Mind and Body

From a Buddhist perspective, good health begins with an understanding of the true nature of the mind–body relationship. Sickness is not merely a physical phenomenon —it can also reflect a spiritual imbalance in our lives.

Buddhism has for thousands of years explained the mind–body relationship in terms remarkably similar to those of current medical research. As outlined by the Chinese teacher T'ien-t'ai (see chapter one), there are five components making each of us unique: (1) form (body), (2) perception, (3) conception, (4) volition and (5) consciousness. We each have a unique form. We each view things subjectively, reaching conclusions quite at odds, at times, with those of others experiencing the same phenomena. Based on these conclusions, we take action. All of this is greatly influenced by the degree to which we are aware of the reality of things.

For example, a woman walking down a dark lane late at night spots a gossamer-white object in a tree. Quickly she realizes what it is and thinks, "Oh, look, someone's laundry got stuck." Moments later, a man comes upon the same tree in the dark and is severely startled thinking he's seen a ghost, has a heart attack and drops dead. What killed him? Surely not the laundry in the tree. It was his misperception of the situation, the conclusion that he was dangerously threatened, a desire to flee with a sudden rise in adrenaline and blood pressure and the effect of all this on his physical well-being.

In Buddhism we seek to replace a distorted view of life with wisdom. As Daisaku Ikeda has written in *Unlocking the Mysteries of Birth and Death*:

> The manifestation of the Buddha nature in one's way of living blocks out the appearance of the negative and destructive tendencies that originate in earthly desires and enables one to harmoniously unify the four spiritual functions of perception, conception, volition and consciousness. Further, manifesting the Buddha nature in one's own life creates harmony on the plane of form and, through the correct balance of the four elements, one's life is able to attain vibrancy and strength. This is the Buddhist ideal of good health.

In other words, as we chant Nam-myoho-renge-kyo, we bring forth from our lives the Buddha condition, which is filled with wisdom and compassion. We can then reflect positively on our beliefs and our actions, which enables us to adjust and reform our lives. We can break the negative karmic chain of thought and action, thereby setting a positive and life-affirming direction. Our life-condition moves from negative to positive tendencies.

Having a healthy life-condition is basic to having a healthy body and mind. Nichiren wrote, "Oneness of body and mind is an ultimate way of life."

The key, then, lies in ridding ourselves of our attachment to deluded or non-life-affirming views. Again, to quote Nichiren: "Therefore, you must quickly reform the tenets that you hold in your heart and embrace the one true vehicle, the single good doctrine [of the Lotus Sutra].... If you do so, then your body will find peace and security and your mind will be calm and untroubled."

Grappling with the delusions that weaken our ability to fight disease is essential to developing and maintaining good health. While science is beginning to recognize the relationship between our spiritual outlook and our health, Buddhism has been dealing with this idea for thousands of years. Its conclusion is that we can bring forth healing medicine from our own lives.

Locked within you are the great treasures of the Buddha nature—wisdom, compassion and courage. When you turn to this medicine cabinet, you truly are the Buddha in the mirror. In medical terms, every human being is both a pharmaceutical manufacturing plant—able to create the medicines needed to ward off illness—and a repository for all of the positive human emotions that affect our ability to fight illness. The key to opening this repository? Chanting Nam-myoho-renge-kyo.

Albert's Experience: Victory Over HIV— A Medical Mystery

The evening of February 20, 1986, is one that Albert will never forget. On his way home from work, he stopped to pick up some groceries. Leaving the store, he was mugged and stabbed twice in the thigh and once in the neck with a hypodermic needle. All for five dollars and some change.

He was taken to the hospital where his wounds were dressed. Since he had been stabbed with a needle, his doctor was aware of the potential for HIV infection but could do no more than encourage him to take care of his health and get regular checkups.

Thirteen years later, HIV showed up in his blood. When he was told this, he was filled with fear and worried whether he could handle the disease. How long would he live? Could he take medication and deal with the side effects?

In the years since the attack, he had begun to practice Nichiren Buddhism. Now he chanted more intensely for his physical health and well-being. The constant encouragement of fellow Buddhists spurred him to make concerted efforts in his own practice through which he sustained confidence, courage and the spirit to challenge his illness. Though of course there were dark times, Albert remained positive and hopeful. He was determined to overcome his illness.

Eventually, he was diagnosed with full-blown AIDS and soon after was hospitalized for pneumonia. His weight dropped from 160 to 119 pounds. His doctor started him on three medications. He did his own research and began to eat healthily and drink various herb teas that minimized his side effects. During this difficult period, he told his doctor that he had two goals: to regain his weight of 160 pounds and to decrease his viral load (the amount of HIV virus in the body) to an undetectable level within two months. His doctor advised him that it would take six to eight months minimum—if he lived that long. He continued to fight the illness using his Buddhist practice. To achieve his goal, he chanted no less than one hour a day, attended Buddhist meetings and studied the writings and teachings of Nichiren every evening. Through these actions, he gained increasing confidence and felt determined to change his condition. Also, he developed a larger purpose in getting well — to prove to others they could do the same. He felt a new control over his destiny. Fellow members rallied to his side, chanting many hours with him throughout this period.

Three months later, he took another blood test. His viral load was indeed undetectable! He weighed in at 140 pounds. Five months after that, the viral load was still undetectable, and his weight was up to 163. Three different doctors told him that this was medically impossible. Yet it happened. Albert had no doubt that his Buddhist practice saved his life, giving him the inner strength and determination, against enormous odds, to fight and win.

Resisting Stress

Are positive emotions really that important in the struggle between health and illness? Is there scientific

evidence to support what Buddhism strongly pro-
pounds? There is a mountain of evidence — and it's
growing rapidly. Let's consider an example.

In the *American Journal of Community Psychology* 6,
psychologist Barbara Dohrenwend describes three ways
that people react to occurrences of stress: (1) Psychological growth as a result of a stressful life event, where
a person matures, changes values and aspirations or
learns new behavior that will help in coping with similar events to come; (2) No substantial permanent psychological change — the person simply resumes life with
no noticeable difference; and (3) The development of a
persistent psychopathology involving maladaptive ways
of coping.

According to Dohrenwend, those most vulnerable to
a maladaptive outcome are likely to feel that the resources available either within themselves or within their
environment are insufficient to handle the demands of
the stressful event. In Buddhist terms, a "maladaptive
outcome" is a behavior based on the delusion that we
are helpless to effect change in our circumstances.

It is important to note Dohrenwend's point that one
possible result of an illness is positive psychological
growth. How we respond to illness determines whether
we are better because of it, unchanged or defeated by it.

Several personality traits (beliefs and attitudes) have been identified that can facilitate the process of handling stress positively. Kathleen H. Dockett, a professor of psychology at the University of the District of Columbia, writes in her booklet *Resources for Stress Resistance: Parallels in Psychology and Buddhism*, of the identification of "a personality style of stress resistance consisting of three factors: commitment, control, and challenge. Essentially, hardy persons are those who are (1) deeply committed to themselves and the activities within their daily lives, (2) believe they can control the events they experience, and (3) view life as an exciting challenge for further growth instead of as a threat."

Dockett concludes that these qualities are among those identified and nurtured by Buddhist practice, qualities stored in the treasure tower called human life. Thus, Dockett writes:

The Buddhism of Shakyamuni, from which Nichiren Daishonin culled the highest teachings, the Lotus Sutra, began 3,000 years ago in India, and psychology a little over 100 years ago. Yet, the profound wisdom of Buddhism has long known and utilized what psychological research has only recently validated to be sound approaches to the development of psychological well-being. This precedent strongly suggests that Buddhism has much to offer within the realm of developing human potentialities, certainly far beyond the topic of stress resistance.

Steve's Experience:
Overcoming Hodgkin's Disease

Just after turning forty, Steve, who had been healthy all his life, suddenly experienced a rapid deterioration in his health. His symptoms included severe back pain, sweating, chills, nausea and fatigue. He was diagnosed with fourth-stage Hodgkin's lymphoma and given a dismal prognosis.

Cancerous tumors had formed behind his ear, on both sides of his neck, and in his sternum and abdomen. A golf-ball-sized tumor was fused into his spine. A team of oncologists recommended a six-cycle regimen of aggressive chemotherapy. He had been practicing Buddhism for some thirteen years. He knew he was in a life-and-death battle with both his illness and the side effects of chemo, and he began vigorously to chant Nam-myoho-renge-kyo each morning and evening to bolster his immune system.

Four months into treatment, his condition worsened.

Suffering from a high fever and compromised immune system, he was hospitalized. Feeling that death was rapidly approaching, he began to chant Nam-myoho-renge-kyo with all the strength he had left.

Early in the morning of the second day of hospitalization, after many, many hours of chanting, his fever broke and he felt revitalized. Several days later, he was given a CT scan. Amazingly, there was no evidence of cancer.

He has been cancer-free and in perfect health since 1987. The team of doctors who worked on his case was deeply impressed by his ability to strengthen his immune system through the practice of Nichiren Buddhism and rid his body of the cancer.

Who Heals?

Many of us feel that treatment of illnesses should be left entirely up to doctors. While it is true that we should trust doctors to help us, if we place too much trust in the power of others, we take the very serious risk of losing power ourselves, of weakening our inner strength. We can best respond to illness by realizing that we ourselves are not only the patient but the doctor as well. Buddhism asks us to be an excellent patient, to find excellent doctors, and to create a unified team. But we are the captains of our own health.

Ultimately, according to Buddhism, what heals our sickness is our life force. Good doctors and excellent medicine can support that function, but they cannot replace it. And chanting Nam-myoho-renge-kyo is the source of this life force. Nam-myoho-renge-kyo is said to be the best medicine ever discovered by human beings, and a Buddha is the best doctor.

Shakyamuni relates a parable that is found in the Lotus Sutra, titled "The Skilled Physician and His Sick Children," which illustrates this truth.

An excellent physician, upon returning home after traveling abroad, finds his many children have taken poison and are writhing in pain on the floor. He quickly prepares excellent medicine that will relieve them of their suffering and offers it to them. Some, rejoicing that their father has returned, quickly take the medicine and are cured. Others, however, are delirious from pain, do not recognize their father and reject the medicine. It is only when they finally recognize him and take the medicine that they, too, are relieved of their suffering.

We can interpret the physician as the Buddha, while we are the children writhing in pain and suffering from the poisons of greed, anger and foolishness. According to Nichiren, the excellent medicine is the chanting of Nam-myoho-renge-kyo. All who take the medicine can overcome the sufferings of this life.

Awakening our innate Buddhahood heals sicknesses in both body and mind. Moreover, the Buddha wisdom we tap through chanting Nam-myoho-renge-kyo can help us to maintain good health or recover it.

Susan's Experience:
Good Health Begins With Self-Love

Susan was raised in a family with an alcoholic father and an unstable mother. She suffered sexual and physical abuse and grew up with little self-esteem. Still in her teens, she left home to escape but almost immediately found herself in an abusive relationship trying to care for her two small children. She left again. Her lack of self-esteem became self-hatred. She became addicted to crack cocaine. Her children were placed in foster care. She would and did do anything to get high, to forget her life of misery and self-loathing. The very idea of self-love was unknown to her. Not surprisingly she was deeply depressed.

Susan was living in this wretched state when she was introduced by a family member to Nichiren Buddhism and began her practice. Although the process did not happen overnight, her Buddhist study and constant chanting of Nam-myoho-renge-kyo gradually fostered a determination within her to love herself. She began to value herself and her children.

It was not easy. She had never had anyone in her immediate environment who was supportive of her, but suddenly she was surrounded with people and a philosophy constantly affirming her fundamental Buddhahood. She chanted for self-esteem. She chanted to love herself and not allow herself to be treated in degrading ways. She made efforts to help others, in spite of feeling inadequate to the task.

From that beginning, she kicked her drug habit and established some stability in her life. She determined that her karma to attract abuse would stop with her and not be passed on to her children, as is all too often the case. Her Buddhist practice has helped her break a chain of suffering that has been passed on for many generations.

Unlocking the Power Within

Among the many positive functions of chanting Nam-myoho-renge-kyo, the Mystic Law, in terms of health, are the following:

The Mystic Law has the power to open the self. Buddhism teaches that one originally possesses an infinite reservoir of energy within. How to open or tap it is the biggest issue. To this end, Nichiren presented us with a key to unlock this energy. Chanting Nam-myoho-renge-kyo enables us to open every potential hidden in the depths of our lives. This has been Buddhism's greatest discovery. It opens the treasure reservoir within, giving us access to unlimited potential.

The Mystic Law has the power to revitalize. Chanting Nam-myoho-renge-kyo brings up life force from within. It can be a healing power in and of itself. It has the power to revitalize, refresh, even reunify and restructure our lives. Through chanting Nam-myoho-renge-kyo, a new life becomes possible. The energy gained from chanting and the positive changes we can effect through it are revolutionary. The practice of Buddhism brings about one's human revolution, which is exactly what is meant by "attaining Buddhahood." Buddhist practice revitalizes our lives as our treasures fill us from within.

The Mystic Law has the power to endow. Hence, anything that is necessary for our happiness will become ours. Health is one of the many endowments or benefits that we can experience through chanting Nam-myoho-renge-kyo.

Ikeda writes: "In short, then, these three functions of the Mystic Law are: to activate our inherent life force, to harmonize our spiritual and physical functions, and to equip us with the resources to influence our environment for the better while responding to its myriad changes with wisdom and maintaining a balance between it and ourselves. When we base our lives on this Law we can tap the limitless power inside ourselves, so that disease is rendered no longer a matter for despair. In fact, the opposite is true: Empowered by the Mystic Law we can transform disease into a source of joy and fulfillment."

The power of our lives can be infinite. The power unleashed through chanting is the ultimate healing power. This is the explosion of healing energy from within. Healing energy also has the power to return one's life to its original form.

Chant Nam-myoho-renge-kyo. Tap into life's enormous potentialities. Gather your inner resources in the battle against illness. This is the Buddhist path to long life and good health.

SEVEN

DEALING
WITH
DEATH

Whereas earlier ages were forthright
in discussing death but reticent about sex,
this age is loquacious to the point
of tedium about sex but flinches from
dealing with death as a fact of life.

—George F. Will

I'm not afraid of death. I just don't want
to be there when it happens.

—Woody Allen

WHEN WE COME to the Buddhist view of death, we tend to think immediately of reincarnation —of being reborn as someone else (richer and better looking, we hope), or perhaps coming back as an animal or even as an insect, depending on how virtuous or vile we have been in life. This is a popular view, but it is almost a cartoon version of Buddhist thought. The followers of Nichiren, numbering more than twelve million worldwide, seldom if ever sit around discussing their past lives.

Buddhism is reason, and the practice of Buddhism requires no outrageous leaps of faith. Logically, no one can know what happens after death, because no one comes back to tell us about it. So the subject of reincarnation remains in the realm of the mystical: that which, at this point in the development of human knowledge and science, cannot be fully understood or explained. It is important, therefore, to emphasize that it is not necessary to believe in reincarnation to begin a Buddhist practice.

While the specific details of rebirth, in what form and when, are ultimately unknowable, the Buddhism described in this book stresses the importance of seeing the big picture — discovering the eternity of life within oneself. In this Buddhism, the challenge presented by the issue of death is to find the most valuable way to live.

Since we all must die eventually, what is the point of living? If we have lived before, why can't we remember our past lives? If life is eternal, in what form will we continue to exist beyond our death?

Buddhism answers these important questions in a way that is at least capable of erasing the fear of death and perhaps even allows confidence in the face of it. Buddhism started by addressing the issue of human suffering. However, Buddhism does not talk about suffering to darken our hearts. Rather it addresses this difficult issue to enlighten us. The primary subjects Shakyamuni Buddha considered were the four universal sufferings of birth (i.e., day-to-day existence), old age, sickness and death. No human being is exempt from these sources of pain. It can be said that the last three sufferings are essentially about the ultimate suffering of death.

As Daisaku Ikeda wrote: "It is only man who becomes

conscious of his death long before dying, and it is only he who has the privilege of living with this awareness. All other beings are equally mortal, but they come to their death with only the briefest awareness of this reality. In this respect, man is endowed with a special prerogative for apprehending his own death, and, because of that, it can paralyze him with fear and worry."

No living thing can escape death. Death can cast a gloomy shadow over the human heart, often reminding us of the finite nature of existence. However unlimited our wealth or fame may seem to be, no matter how enduring our love or relationships, the reality of our eventual demise can undermine our sense of well-being. For many, the fear of death is deep-seated. It can weaken the foundations of our lives, cause worries, suffering and torment. At the same time, if the basis of our lives is shaky, various spiritual and emotional problems can become manifest. Here we see a vicious circle in the mind and heart caused by the apprehensions of death. Nichiren understood that our fear of death profoundly affects our health and happiness. He wrote, "We should first learn about the issue of dying and then study all other affairs."

Shakyamuni's quest for enlightenment is said to have been motivated by a desire to find a solution to the four fundamental sufferings and, more specifically, by a desire to overcome the fear of death. And it was the problem of death—how to cope with it and transcend it—that inspired the creation of many other religious and philosophical systems.

Confrontation with death has been called the mother of philosophy. The German existentialist Martin Heidegger termed human existence itself a "being-unto-death," since man carries within him the knowledge of his impending demise from an early age. Hence the Buddhist saying, "The cause of death is not disease, but birth." It might seem preferable not to think about death, except perhaps at the very end of our lives. Yet now, due to advances in medical science, the time people spend fighting face to face against death has lengthened considerably. The agony and uncertainty stretch out for months, even years. This has brought with it a corresponding societal reevaluation of death in medical and ethical terms, with social effects ranging from the hospice movement to the debate over voluntary euthanasia. Yet, for all our medical advances, we still cannot agree when life begins—or ends.

Much of the uncertainty and instability we see in contemporary society can be traced to a lack of understanding about death. The feeling that our lives are finite

—that the moment of physical death means, with absolute finality, the end of our existence — gives rise to a kind of desperate urgency in life. When you feel that "you only live once," there is a temptation to cram as many pleasures and sensations into the limited time available to you. As the saying goes, "Eat, drink and be merry, for tomorrow we die." In today's time-starved society, every imaginable gadget and service has been dreamed up to save precious seconds of time so that we can enjoy a few more fun-filled moments of "leisure." A grim workaholism by day often gives way to a full-blown hedonism after hours. It is no surprise that the pursuit of pleasure has come to take on a frenetic quality, and the drive to acquire material wealth has become a virtual obsession. Too often life becomes subordinated to careerism and the drive for success. However, at the moment of death, few people look back over their lives and say, "I should have spent more time in the office."

From the standpoint of a society firmly grounded in materialism, death is the final denial of all our material attributes, so we fear it inordinately, just as we fear the loss of our material possessions during our lifetime. As a result, we escape into secularism, making no attempt to examine the inner life of the mind or the nature of death, living life only for the moment. What is death?

What becomes of us after we die? Failing to pursue these questions is like spending our student years never considering what to do after graduating. Without coming to terms with death, we cannot establish a strong direction in life. Pursuing this issue brings real stability and depth to our lives.

Is there a view of death and what lies beyond that contains a spiritual dimension but does not contradict the known scientific laws of the universe? Indeed there is. Buddhism puts forth a naturalistic, as opposed to a supernaturalistic, view of death. Let's explain what we mean by this.

The Buddhist View of Life and Death

For many people, death signifies the mere absence of life. In this view, life is perceived as all that is good — that which embodies fullness and light. Death is perceived as all that is bad — all that connotes emptiness and darkness. This negative perception of death has influenced human existence since the dawn of history. But this notion is a simplistic, childlike view of the reality of death, especially when you consider death in terms of the cycles of creation and extinction that govern the natural world, even the universe itself. As we have seen,

Buddhism teaches with great specificity the intimate and inseparable relationship between the microcosm of the individual human being and the macrocosm of the universe. All universal phenomena are contained in a single moment of life, in the depths of our lives, and each moment of life vibrates in rhythm with all phenomena in the universe. This is not an insight limited to the followers of Nichiren or any other school of philosophy. In this connection, the words of the poet William Blake strike a Buddhistic chord:

To see a World in a grain of sand,
And a Heaven in a wild flower,
Hold Infinity in the palm of your hand,
And Eternity in an hour.

To have such perceptions is truly to live *in* the moment, as opposed to *for* the moment. It is the difference between the material and the eternal. Buddhism views our lives in the context of the macrocosm, the life of the universe, which has existed throughout eternity (or at least from the unimaginably distant past). Likewise, our lives, which are one with this universe, have also always existed in one form or another, following an unending cycle of birth and death, decline and renewal, subject to the physical laws of this universe. According to the Buddha's teaching, life, like energy, can be neither created nor destroyed, and what appears to be death is merely the process of decline and renewal that governs all things. Thus Buddhist philosophy anticipates by nearly three thousand years the laws of conservation of energy and matter, which state that neither energy nor matter are ever lost but merely converted into different forms. (For example, the electrical energy that passes through a light bulb is converted into heat and light.) Nichiren taught that life and death are alternating aspects of our real selves, as expressed by the law of Nam-myoho-renge-kyo. He wrote:

> *Myo* represents death, and *ho*, life. Living beings that pass through the two phases of life and death are the entities of the Ten Worlds, or the entities of Myoho-renge-kyo…. No phenomena — either heaven or earth, yin or yang, the sun or the moon, the five planets [In the thirteenth century only Mercury, Venus, Mars, Jupiter and Saturn had been discovered, Ed.] , or any of the worlds from hell to Buddhahood — are free from the two phases of life and death. Life and death are simply the two functions of Myoho-renge-kyo.

In other words, all things that physically manifest themselves in life withdraw into a state of latency upon their extinction or death. Buddhism distinguishes between physical reality and a state of latency wherein life continues to exist unseen. This latency, a state of neither existence nor nonexistence, can be confusing to Westerners. To us, something either exists or it does not. But think of a cherry blossom in winter. While the flower is not visible, it is there, dormant, waiting to bloom when the right conditions (spring) present themselves. The same is true of our lives. When the physical body ceases to function, our lives enter a new phase, a period of dormancy, followed by rebirth. As Daisaku Ikeda wrote:

According to the Buddhist view, life is eternal. It is believed to undergo successive incarnations, so that death is thought to be not so much the cessation of an existence as the beginning of a new one. For Buddhists the phenomenon of transmigration is self-evident—as, indeed, it was to the ancient Indians, who gave it the Sanskrit name *samsara*. The fundamental premise of Buddhism is that life is eternal and that individual living beings undergo a continuing cycle of birth and death. Some of the findings of recent scientific research in the fields of both medicine and parapsychology tend to support this view. These researches include studies of "near-death experiences" and "past-life experiences."

While the revival of a philosophical perspective oriented toward eternal life may seem idealistic or unscientific — a mere emotional balm to our existential dread — in truth, it is the most reasonable, realistic way to look at the matter. Without death, there would be no life. Josei Toda, the second president of the Soka Gakkai, once wrote:

Nothing would be more fearful than not to die. It would be one thing if there were only human beings. But if all living beings were not to die, the consequences would be truly calamitous. Suppose that cats and dogs and mice and even octopuses all were not to die. This would create great problems. If nothing were to die, then what would happen? Even if someone or something were beaten, or killed, or run over by a train, or deprived of food, it would not die. The results would be pandemonium.

Death is necessary. Because we die, we can appreciate the wonder of life. We can savor the great joy of being alive. Nichiren grasped the profound concept of life and death as expressed by the Lotus Sutra, that both life and death are inherent in human life. He pointed out that people's view of life and death as separate phenomena leads to a belief either in eternalism, the idea that the soul exists forever, or annihilation, the idea that there is nothing beyond death. In Hamlet's famous words, "the rest is silence." Both perspectives, Nichiren said, are deluded, because they ignore the cycle of life and death permeating the universe. As he wrote:

> To hate life and death and try to separate oneself from them is delusion or partial enlightenment. To perceive life and death as essential is enlightenment or total realization. Now, when Nichiren and his disciples chant Nam-myoho-renge-kyo, they know that life and death are intrinsic workings of the fundamental essence. Being and nonbeing, birth and death, appearance and disappearance, worldly existence and future extinction—all are essential and everlasting processes.

It is by deeply understanding this sophisticated view that we can advance toward enlightenment and experience death with dignity. But the question remains, if life goes on, in what form does it continue? Since form implies shape or substance, and Buddhist teaching does not suggest that the physical self somehow survives and is reborn, another approach is needed. To fully understand death from a Buddhist perspective, we must delve into what is called "the nine consciousnesses."

The Nine Levels of Consciousness

The Buddhist theory of the nine consciousnesses is a psychological system that has often been compared to the pioneering work of Swiss psychologist Carl Jung, who postulated a "collective unconscious" of memories common to all human beings. These memories come from the distant past and contain archetypal images that occur in all cultures and have been passed down from prehistoric times. Jung's idea of a collective unconscious is analogous to the eighth, or *alaya,* consciousness in Buddhist theory, which acts as a storehouse for memories collected by the first seven consciousnesses — and survives after death.

According to the Buddhist analysis, the first five consciousnesses correspond to the five senses of sight, hearing, smell, taste and touch. The sixth consciousness integrates the perception of the five senses into coherent images and makes judgments about the external world. For example, take a rose petal. It is red, soft and fragrant. Our sixth consciousness compiles these sensory data and comes up with the idea of a rose, as opposed to, say, a strawberry. Together, the first six consciousnesses form the conscious mind.

In contrast to the first six consciousnesses, which deal with the external world, the seventh, or *mano*-consciousness, does not rely directly on the senses. It discerns the inner world. From the seventh consciousness comes the considered judgment: A rose is quite beautiful. Awareness of and attachment to the self are said to originate from the *mano*-consciousness, as does the capacity to distinguish between good and evil. Here, *mano* means "to discern." In terms of Freudian psychology, it might be considered similar to the ego. It was through his grasp of the seventh consciousness that the French philosopher René Descartes could formulate the famous proof of his own existence, "I think, therefore I am." When we are awake, the realm of the six senses is dominant. When we are asleep, the hidden seventh consciousness surfaces in the form of dreams, while the functions of the six senses become latent.

The eighth level, the *alaya*-consciousness, is a step deeper than the *mano*-consciousness, or the realm of individual ego. All the functions of our six senses as reactions, to outer stimulation and our judgments about them, even our most fleeting impressions, are stored and recorded in the eighth consciousness. This storehouse is roughly comparable to memory, but it is also more than that. Buddhism suggests that the eighth consciousness remembers and stores not only everything we have experienced in this life—including all the causes we have made through thoughts, words and actions—but also everything we have experienced in the remote past.

Buddhism teaches that there is no such thing as a soul or spirit that governs one's body and mind and continues to exist, floating in the air, after one's death. Christianity and other Western religions hold that a person lives only once, and actions taken during this limited span determine forever the fate of an eternal soul. It is as if life were a book that is read through only once. In the Buddhist view, to use the same metaphor, life is like a page in a book. When one turns the page, a new one appears.

Instead of an ethereal soul, Buddhism espouses the notion of a true self, which continues to exist whether one is alive or deceased. The *alaya*-consciousness may be thought of as the realm that interweaves all the causes and effects constituting the destiny of this individual self. When this life reappears in the phenomenal world, the karmic seeds in the *alaya*-consciousness bloom once again, but in new conditions and in a new physical form. One's self continues throughout eternity. Buddhism accepts this as fact. Whether dormant in death or manifest in living, it's the same life energy.

Consider this: Whether you are two, seventeen, fifty-two or seventy-eight years old, you are the same person. Even though, as medical science tells us, nearly every cell in your body will have replaced itself during your life span, you are still you. Your personality may have changed radically. You may have changed careers, political persuasions, and so on. But there is something continuous that exists throughout the depths of your life. It is the essence of you. All of the memories, habits and karma stored in the *alaya*-consciousness as time goes by form the individual self, or the framework of individual being that repeats the cycle of death and rebirth.

There is nothing static or irreversible about this karma or inherited consciousness. No matter what our karma, we can change it for the better using our free will. In other words, the Buddhist concept of karma is in no way what is ordinarily called fate or destiny. Some people labor under the illusion of fatalism, seeing only one aspect of karma, that the karma from one's past lives is continued in one's present life. However, according to the law of causality, at each moment we create fresh karma. This means that at the current moment also, of our own free will, we are creating a new life tendency and opening up the future. Nichiren said that in the eternal cycle of life and death, the law of cause and effect is an iron rule. With an awareness that we can find positive meaning in whatever happens in life, chanting Nam-myoho-renge-kyo is the way to improve or change one's karma.

When we recognize that the essential causes and conditions of our happiness lie within our own lives, we can summon the courage to find ourselves responsible for our sufferings and exert every possible effort to change them and create happiness. As we begin to understand that we are the creators of our own destiny, we find in ourselves a star of hope that illuminates every aspect of existence.

After death, however, in this new existence, despite having our karmic "memory" intact, we will have no conscious memory of our previous life. As the Miscellaneous Agama Sutra states, "The karmic effects exist, but the person who caused them no longer." In effect, one is forced to drink the waters of Lethe, the river that makes one forget the past in Greek mythology. As modern neuroscience has well established, physical memory needs a physical brain, and the brain that remembers incidents of this life is different from the consciousness that registered the events of the life before. When the physical brain dies, so do its memories. The karmic memory that we call *alaya*, upon which is etched all the causes we have made, is different in kind from the brain. But the underlying self is the same. Just as no period of sleep, no matter how long and deep, can alter our identity, our karma lives on.

The nature of that which is reborn has been the subject of endless futile discussion. When one candle is lighted from another, is the light from the second the same as the light from the first? But the details are not important in the quest for enlightenment. The theory of the nine consciousnesses is, after all, a theory. But it is an uncannily compelling one in the light of what is now known about the universe, human nature and psychology. According to this theory, the *alaya*-consciousness, which functions as the basis of all emotional and spiritual functions, is in constant flux, like a rushing torrent unceasingly undergoing transitions and transformations. This dynamic state at the fundamental level of life maintains the unique characteristics of each individual life. When we are awake, it lies buried beneath the surface, giving rise to vague feelings, helping us to form hunches,

and powerfully influencing our likes and dislikes. When
we sleep, the first six consciousnesses recede, and the
mano-consciousness takes over. That doesn't mean that
our senses are completely shut off. A loud noise or a
bright light can certainly awaken us. When we die, however, our lives revert entirely to the realm of *alaya*-con-
sciousness. Therefore, we don't see, we don't hear, we
don't smell, we don't taste, and we don't feel by touch-
ing. One's consciousness goes beyond even the seventh
consciousness and wholly into the *alaya*.

The analogy between sleep and death (the "big
sleep") is compelling. As British author and Buddhist
leader Richard Causton wrote in his book, *The Buddha
in Daily Life*:

> Sleep, like death, is a fundamental and mysterious
> aspect of all life. We go to bed tired and awake
> refreshed. Buddhism teaches that we die when we
> are worn-out, and our life entity is then reborn
> anew. Both sleep and death thus express the con-
> tinual rhythm and energy of *myoho*, the Mystic Law.
> The lesson here is clear, for when we are truly able
> to regard death as we regard sleep, as a period of
> rest and recuperation in our eternal lives, it will cer-
> tainly hold no terror for us. Indeed, we can even

look forward to it as we look forward to a good night's sleep after a hard day's work, confident that our lives will make a fresh and vigorous start next time around.

Researchers have demonstrated that there are different levels of sleep. During the stage of REM (rapid eye movement), the brain-wave patterns are especially intense and interrupted dreams can be readily recalled. According to Causton, Buddhism regards dreaming as the various thoughts, words and deeds stored in the eighth consciousness becoming "liberated" as the conscious mind releases its hold for a few hours. A person awakened from REM sleep is immediately aware of his surroundings. Whereas someone awakened from the deepest realms of slumber, or delta sleep, can experience extreme disorientation and memory dysfunction. A highly suggestive passage from Marcel Proust's *Remembrance of Things Past* illustrates this point:

But for me it was not enough if, in my own bed, my sleep was so heavy as completely to relax my consciousness; for then I lost all sense of the place in which I had gone to sleep, and when I awoke in the middle of the night, not knowing where I was,

I could not even be sure at first who I was; I had only the most rudimentary sense of existence; such as may lurk and flicker in the depths of an animal's consciousness; I was more destitute than the cave-dweller; but then the memory—not yet of the place in which I was, but of various other places where I had lived and might now very possibly be—would come like a rope let down from heaven to draw me up out of the abyss of not-being, from which I could never have escaped by myself: in a flash I would traverse centuries of civilization, and out of a blurred glimpse of oil-lamps, then of shirts with turned-down collars, would gradually piece together the original components of my ego.

This state of "not-being" so eloquently described by Proust suggests the existence of a level of consciousness even deeper than that experienced during regular dreaming. It is similar to the documented experiences of people who have come back from the brink of death. Near-death experiences, with their vividly consistent reports of observing one's body in a serene and detached way, suggest that one's self, even though the body has virtually expired, still remains alive. In Buddhist tales, a deceased person typically crosses a river, which indicates the passage from *mano*-consciousness to the *alaya*-consciousness. These experiences and tales point to the notion that, at the depths of this rushing torrent of *alaya*-consciousness, there is a pure and peaceful reservoir, the eternal and unchanging Buddha nature.

The Ninth Consciousness, or Buddhahood

It can be said that the reason Buddhist teaching can put death into perspective is that it discovered the ultimate realm within one's life that is free from all karmic impurity. This is called the *amala*-consciousness, or enlightenment. *Amala* here means absolute purity. It is a realm connected directly with the life of the universe, which is understood to be Nam-myoho-renge-kyo, the ultimate law of life and death. Nichiren also called this realm "the palace of the ninth consciousness." Both life and death are natural expressions of human existence, and both are incorporated in the great universal life of Buddhahood that exists in the depths of our lives. By basing ourselves upon our Buddhahood established through Buddhist practice in this lifetime, we experience death in this lifetime with dignity and peace.

Referring to the death of the father of a young believer, Nichiren wrote: "When he was alive, he was a Buddha in life, and now he is a Buddha in death. He is a Buddha in both life and death. This is what is meant by that most important doctrine called attaining Buddhahood in one's present form."

In this short passage, Nichiren teaches the principle that we can be happy eternally by attaining Buddhahood in this lifetime. The ultimate message of the Lotus Sutra is that Buddhahood exists as a potential within everyone. Nichiren presented the way to reveal it from within and taught us the way to solidify it in us as well. Thus, if we have tapped into the ultimate depths of life, Buddhahood, while alive, the flow thus begun continues through death and into the next life.

Through practicing his teaching (chanting Nam-myoho-renge-kyo) we can develop the wisdom and conviction to put death into perspective. By continually enlightening ourselves, we can also establish an unshakable confidence in the eternity of our lives. Furthermore, by practicing Nichiren's teaching, we can experience an upsurge of joy from within. And, finally, since fearlessness is an aspect of Buddhahood, fear of death is something we *can* conquer. Only then can we focus on what we are supposed to do with the rest of our lives for the happiness of all humanity, thus fulfilling our mission in this life and in this world.

In *Unlocking the Mysteries of Birth and Death*, Daisaku Ikeda wrote:

[Nichiren] gave concrete expression to the *amala-*consciousness—the fundamental reality of life—in the phrase Nam-myoho-renge-kyo, and he gave physical form to his enlightenment to the original cosmic life in the Gohonzon, the object of devotion, thus opening a path whereby all people can achieve Buddhahood, manifesting the greater self that is latent within them. When we devote ourselves to the Gohonzon we find joy and determination welling forth as we are brought face to face with the reality that our own existences are coextensive with the eternal life of the universe. When we devote ourselves to and base our lives on this reality—the *amala*-consciousness—all the other eight consciousnesses work to express the immense power and the infinite wisdom of the Buddha nature.

The Right Way of Dying

As the law of cause and effect requires, we die the way we lived. At the moment of death, our past causes show most plainly in our appearance. At that time there is no way to conceal the truth about the life that has been lived. Therefore, to talk about what is an ideal way to die is really to talk about the ideal way to live. We carry out our Buddhist practice now so that we will not have to experience regret on our deathbeds. The way in which we face the moment of death determines whether or not we have crowned our lives with fulfillment.

Buddhism is a teaching that finds absolute value within the life of each human being. In Buddhism, a person who has made his or her potential blossom fully is, in a sense, a Buddha. A person who has done everything possible to fulfill his or her mission in this lifetime is also called a Buddha. Ikeda wrote:

Death will come to each of us some day. We can die having fought hard for our beliefs and convictions, or we can die having failed to do so. Since the reality of death is the same in either case, isn't it far better that we set out on our journey toward the next existence in high spirits, with a bright smile on our faces, knowing that in everything we did, we did the very best we could, thrilling with the sense "That was truly an interesting life"?

So from a Buddhist perspective, our ability to pass successfully through the dying process depends on our steady efforts during life to accumulate good causes, to contribute to the happiness of others and to strengthen the foundation of goodness and humanity in the depths of our lives. Having thus been a victor in life, we can win in death as well. This is the process of using the law of cause and effect to create ultimate value.

Thus we can see that death is more than the absence of life; that death, together with active life, is necessary for the formation of a larger, more essential whole. This great whole reflects the deeper continuity of life and death that we experience as individuals and express as culture. A central challenge for the new century will be to establish a culture based on an understanding of the relationship of life and death, and of life's essential eternity. Such an attitude does not disown death, but directly confronts and correctly positions it within the larger context of life.

To die happily is difficult. And since death is the final settlement of accounts for one's life, that is when our true self comes to the fore. We practice Buddhism to live happily and to die happily. Buddhism guarantees that those who practice sincerely will approach death in a state of supreme fulfillment.

EIGHT

PUTTING IT ALL INTO PRACTICE

**It is never too late to be
what you might have become.**
—George Eliot

You are all the Buddha.
—said to be the last words of Shakyamuni Buddha

OVER THE COURSE of this book, we've discussed how the key to surmounting life's hurdles and achieving its goals lies within each of us, the Buddhas in our respective mirrors. We've examined the interconnection between ourselves and others, and between our lives and our respective environments. We've even explored how to face death in a fresh, encouraging way. The crucial step now is putting into practice what we've learned, making the thrilling leap from the mere holding of knowledge to the actualization of our vast potential. As we've said, Buddhism is reason, and what's more reasonable than being asked to put stock in something only after we have received proof of its effectiveness?

The primary practice, as we have explained throughout the book, is to chant Nam-myoho-renge-kyo.

The Mechanics of Chanting

Nam-myoho-renge-kyo can be chanted anywhere at any time — preferably in a manner that won't disturb others — but the effects of practice are best seen when carried out on a regular basis. We suggest setting aside a bit of time each morning and evening for, say, at least five minutes each session. Sit straight and comfortably, and, if possible, face a blank portion of the wall or some neutral background that won't distract you. Place your palms together at chest level, fingers pointing upward with the tips at just about the level of your chin.

As to pronunciation:

Nam – the a has the sound of the a in *father*

Myo – think of it as placing an m before one half of *yo-yo*

Ho – like the garden implement *hoe*

Ren – like the bird *wren*

Ge – sounds like the word *get* without the t

Kyo – similar to *myo*

Each syllable gets one equal stress or beat:

Nám myó hó rén gé kyó

The chant repeats without a break between each Nam-myoho-renge-kyo. Feel free, of course, to breathe whenever necessary, then go back to your rhythmic chant. Try to maintain an even tone and rhythm, but don't be overly concerned about it as you will settle into it naturally in a short time. You can either focus on a specific goal or problem, or you can let your mind naturally coast from thought to thought. You will soon see some tangible result.

Again, this is not to say that you must have conviction that this will happen from the very start. It is only natural to have doubt. Confidence in Buddhist practice begins with your very first attempt to "try it and see." And it deepens over time as you gain continual, actual proof. Yet doubt is an element with which practitioners must always contend. As the German author Hermann Hesse said: "Faith and doubt correspond to each other and supplement each other. There is no true faith where there is no doubt."

The essential thing, however, is to use your doubts as fuel to find the answers to your questions. Practically speaking, it helps if you can bolster your practice by relating to like-minded others who can encourage you through life's inevitable rough spots, and whom you can encourage in turn based on your own emerging experiences. As this book has pointed out, we don't live in a vacuum, and our efforts to help others become happy directly enhance our own level of happiness.

If you'd like to take things a step (or thirty-seven) further, there is a vast community of Nichiren Buddhists to
assist you in your great experiment. The SGI-USA holds
discussion meetings and cultural activities in all fifty
states as well as throughout the Caribbean, on Guam
and other Pacific islands. Most meetings are informal
and held in practitioners' homes. Through the community of fellow Buddhists, you can take the next step of
learning about the supplementary practice, the twice-
daily recitation of portions of two chapters of the Lotus
Sutra, which bolsters one's daily chanting of Nam-
myoho-renge-kyo. This aspect of practice requires some
tricky pronunciations, and an experienced guide can be
invaluable. You can also receive the Gohonzon, or "object
of devotion" to focus on while you chant. The Gohonzon
enables you to fuse your subjective wisdom with the
objective reality of the universe (see Chapter 3 for a
detailed explanation).

Having a Buddhist friend to guide you along the way
is exceedingly helpful in maintaining your practice, and
the SGI-USA provides a structure for making just such
a friend (or many!). In fact, through the umbrella organization SGI, you can find friends and activities (some
twelve million practitioners in more than 160 nations)

throughout the world. For information about meetings and activities in your area, you can call the SGI-USA headquarters in Santa Monica, California, at 1-310- 260- 8900. Or visit its website: www.sgi-usa.org

At the beginning of this book, we spoke of each individual's limitless potential for wisdom, courage, hope, confidence, compassion, vitality and endurance. The adventure begins the very first time you chant Nam-myoho-renge-kyo and introduce yourself to the Buddha in your mirror.

Bibliography

Bronowski, Jacob. *The Ascent of Man*. London: BBC Enterprises, 1973.

Causton, Richard. *The Buddha In Daily Life, An Introduction to the Buddhism of Nichiren Daishonin*. London: Rider, 1995.

Derbolav, Josef and Daisaku Ikeda. *Search For A New Humanity*. Translated and edited by Richard L. Gage. New York: Weatherhill, Inc., 1992.

Dockett, Kathleen H. *Resources for Stress Resistance: Parallels in Psychology and Buddhism*. Santa Monica, Calif.: SGI-USA, 1993.

Dohrenwend, Barbara. "Social Stress and Community Psychology." In *American Journal of Community Psychology 6*. New York: Plenum Publishing Corp., 1978.

Humphreys, Christmas. *Buddhism*. 3d ed. Baltimore: Penguin Books, 1962.

Huyghe, Rene and Daisaku Ikeda. *Dawn After Dark*. Translated by Richard L. Gage. New York: Weatherhill, Inc., 1991.

Ikeda, Daisaku, in conversation with Masayoshi Kiguchi and Eiichi Shimura. *Buddhism and the Cosmos*. London: Macdonald & Co., 1985.

——. *Buddhism, the First Millennium*. Tokyo: Kodansha International Ltd., 1977.

——. *Faith into Action*. Santa Monica, Calif.: World Tribune Press, 1999.

——. and Bryan Wilson. *Human Values In a Changing World, A Dialogue on the Social Rôle of Religion*. Secaucus, N.J.: Lyle Stuart Inc., 1987.

——. *The Living Buddha*. New York: Weatherhill, 1976.

——. *My Dear Friends in America*. Santa Monica, Calif.: World Tribune Press, 2001.

——. *A New Humanism*. New York: Weatherhill, Inc., 1996.

——. *Selected Lectures on the Gosho, Vol. 1*. Tokyo: NSIC, 1979.

——. *SGI President Ikeda's Addresses in the United States.* Santa Monica, Calif.: World Tribune Press, 1996.

——. *Unlocking the Mysteries of Birth and Death: Buddhism in the Contemporary World.* London: Macdonald & Co., 1988.

——. *The Way of Youth, Buddhist Common Sense for Handling Life's Questions.* Santa Monica, Calif.: Middleway Press, 2000.

Keller, Helen. *The Story of My Life.* Garden City, N.J.: Doubleday, 1954.

Landes, David S. *The Wealth and Poverty of Nations: Why Some Are Rich and Some So Poor.* New York: W.W. Norton & Co., 1998.

Levi, Sylvain. *L'Inde et le Monde.* Paris: Librairie Ancienne Honor, Champion, 1926.

NSIC. *Fundamentals of Buddhism.* 3d ed. Tokyo: NSIC, 1977.

Pauling, Linus and Daisaku Ikeda. *A Lifelong Quest for Peace.* Translated and edited by Richard L. Gage. Boston: Jones and Bartlett Publishers, 1992.

Peck, M. Scott. *The Road Less Traveled and Beyond: Spiritual Growth in An Age of Anxiety.* New York: Simon & Schuster, 1977.

Proust, Marcel. *Remembrance of Things Past.* Translated by C.K. Scott Moncrieff and Terence Kilmartin. New York: Random House, 1981.

Shaw, George Bernard. *Man and Superman.* London: Penguin Books, 1988.

Toda, Josei. *Lectures on the Sutra.* Tokyo: Seikyo Press, 1967.

Thurman, Robert A. F., Ph.D. "Being Free and Enjoying Life." In *Buddhism in America.* Compiled by Al Rapaport. Edited by Brian D. Hotchkiss. Boston: Tuttle Publishing, 1998.

Toynbee, Arnold and Daisaku Ikeda. *Choose Life, A Dialogue.* London: Oxford University Press, 1976.

Turner, Tina and Kurt Loder. *I, Tina.* New York: Morrow, 1986.

Watson, Burton. *The Lotus Sutra.* New York: Columbia University Press, 1993.

Wickramasinghe, Chandra and Daisaku Ikeda. *Space and Eternal Life.* London: Journeyman Press, 1998.

Index

MORE ON NICHIREN BUDDHISM
AND ITS APPLICATION TO DAILY LIFE

*The Way of Youth: Buddhist Common Sense
for Handling Life's Questions,* by Daisaku Ikeda

"[This book] shows the reader how to flourish as a young person in the world today; how to build confidence and character in modern society; learn to live with respect for oneself and others; how to contribute to a positive, free and peaceful society; and find true personal happiness." —Midwest Book Review (14.95, Middleway Press, ISBN 0-9674697-0-8)

*For the Sake of Peace: Seven Paths to Global Harmony,
A Buddhist Perspective,* by Daisaku Ikeda

"[Ikeda] is a true citizen of the world and peace leader. In *For the Sake of Peace*, he describes a path to peace through individual commitment and self-control, dialogue and the creation of cultures of peace. Recognizing the considerable obstacles to creating a peaceful world, he inspires hope that such a world is possible." —David Krieger, President, Nuclear Age Peace Foundation (25.95, Middleway Press, ISBN 0-9674697-2-4)

*Soka Education: A Buddhist Vision for Teachers,
Students and Parents,* by Daisaku Ikeda

From the Japanese word meaning "to create value," this book presents a fresh spiritual perspective to question the ultimate purpose of education. Mixing American pragmatism with Buddhist philosophy, the goal of Soka education is the lifelong happiness of the learner. Rather than offering practical class-room techniques, this book speaks to the emotional heart of both the teacher and student. (25.95, Middleway Press, ISBN 0-9674697-4-0)

The Living Buddha, An Interpretive Biography, by Daisaku Ikeda

This is a biography with a double focus. It is at once a vivid historical narrative based on what is known or can be reasonably surmised about Shakyamuni Buddha's life and times, and an inspiring account of a heroic life dedicated to helping all people free themselves from suffering. (12.95, Weatherhill, ISBN 0-8348-0322-4)